LIBER TERRIBILIS

FOUNDATIONS OF PRACTICAL SORCERY VOLUME VII

FOUNDATIONS OF PRACTICAL SORCERY VOLUME VII

LIBER TERRIBILIS

BEING AN INSTRUCTION ON THE SEVENTY-TWO SPIRITS OF THE GOETIA

Gary St. M. Nottingham

Published by Avalonia
www.avaloniabooks.co.uk

Published by Avalonia

BM Avalonia
London
WC1N 3XX
England, UK
www.avaloniabooks.co.uk

LIBER TERRIBILIS
Copyright © 2012 G. St. Michael Nottingham
Artwork Frances Mary Nottingham All Hallows 2013

First Edition 2012.
This revised edition, 2015.

All rights reserved.

ISBN 978-1-905297-80-1

Design by Satori, for Avalonia.

British Library Cataloguing in Publication Data. A catalogue record for this book is available from the British Library.

All rights reserved. No part of this publication may be reproduced or utilised in any form or by any means, electronic or mechanical, including photocopying, microfilm, recording, or by any information storage and retrieval system, or used in another book, without written permission from the author.

About the Author

Gary St. M. Nottingham's commitment to the study and practice of the alchemical arte, ritual magic, grimoires and spirit conjuration means that he can often be found peering at bubbling flasks or a shewstone – or otherwise engaged in deepening his knowledge and understanding of such matters. His practices also draw on the work of the 17th-century astrologer William Lilly and the arte of horary astrology.

He organised the legendary Ludlow Esoteric Conference (2004-2008), helped produce Verdelet occult magazine, has taught many free day workshops on basic occult skills and is a popular speaker at esoteric conferences.

The seven volumes of Foundations of Practical Sorcery are an unabridged collection of Gary's much sought-after previously published work, updated and made available to a wider readership at last.

Gary was raised in south Shropshire, where, during his mid-teens, he became involved with a small Coven, thereby gaining an excellent grounding in a wide selection of magical practices. Following the conjuration of a spirit, and asking it for help that manifested when least expected, he subsequently became involved with a group of practising alchemists. He has a background in horticulture, enjoys spending time in the garden and playing chess.

For My Sister & Companion in the Arte FMN

"Glyndwr: *I can call spirits from the vasty deep.*

Hotspur: *Why, so can I, or so can any man;*
But will they come when you do call for them?"

Shakespeare – Henry IV

'And the angel of God which went before the camp of Israel, removed and went behind them, and the pillar of the cloud went from before their face and stood behind them.

And it came between the camp of the Egyptians and the camp of Israel and it was a cloud and darkness to them, but it gave light by night to these: So that one came not near the other all the night.

And Moses stretched out his hand over the sea and the Lord caused the sea to go back by a strong east wind all that night and made the sea dry land and the waters were divided.'

Exodus 14:19-21

Table of Contents

INTRODUCTION 8
PROLOGUE 10

OF OUR ARTE 13
OF THOSE SPIRITS BOTH DARKSOME AND DIVINE 16
ARS PRACTICA 161
OF THE TOOLS OF ARTE 162
OF PREPARATION 175
MODUS OPERANDI 182
SUGGESTED FURTHER READING 192

INDEX 193

Introduction

We live in an age where we are awash with information on all subjects, and to this the magical artes are no exception. Whilst the student of magic can easily access all manner of electronic files there is nothing quite like a book.

A book can not only be picked up and read, but will, in many instances, over time, become a friend, guide and teacher who has assisted the reader on their journey throughout their life. Quite simply books can change lives and this is why those who have been in positions of power through the centuries have tried, and often failed, to keep knowledge out of the hands of everyday folk. This is perhaps primarily because they feared the power of the book to cause change, and change is what the seven books in the Foundations of Practical Sorcery series will cause.

Today the magical artes have never been so accessible, although that doesn't mean the demands that the arte makes upon the practitioner have been lessened in any way. While the arte is, in principle, for all, not everyone will have the self-discipline, the will and the imagination to succeed therein. However for those who do have these basic attributes or are prepared to acquire them there is much to be gained from the practice of magic in all levels of life. For many people their ingress into the arte will be by books, and the exploration of and working with the information they contain. There is nothing like experience even if your magic proves less successful than hoped for: there is no such thing as failure in magic, because every experience will, at the very least, teach the practitioner something, even if it's just to try harder next time!

Of course some will have access to a magical group and the knowledge and collective experience to be found therein; but for many this will not be the case. Magical groups regardless of hue by and large have much to commend them, but not all of them do. I have in the past been approached by people who have gone through a coven system yet then been led to ask me to help them practice and study magic. It seemed their coven did not in fact practice the arte; which left me wondering what was it that they did do. I am aware of similar approaches made to other magical practitioners, which has left me concluding that some magical groups and covens can actually be detrimental to an individual's magical development and understanding - although this is certainly not the case with all by any means.

Foundations of Practical Sorcery goes some way to rectifying this deficit in any student's magical life. They offer clear magical instruction and accounts of magical acts to be performed, thus making the arte easily accessible. The methods and techniques presented are all based upon my own personal knowledge and experience which goes back over forty years, methods and techniques that have worked successfully for me and will do so for any reader who applies them accordingly.

In many ways I was fortunate, during the autumn of 1972, to meet a magical practitioner who taught me much regarding the arte, generously affording me the run of their magical library as well. Having been schooled extensively in magical knowledge from my mid teen years I consider myself to have been extremely fortunate and lucky to have had many experiences not easily available to many people. Thus the present Foundations of Practical Sorcery series is the distillation of four decades of successful magical workings.

Each of the seven volumes gives a clear account and rendition of one or another area of magical instruction that I have received and have been taught. They are presented to the reader in a clear and workable style which will provide them with a concise and firm foundation, allowing the serious magical student to explore the Western Magical Tradition, the inheritance of us all.

Gary St. M. Nottingham, February 2015

Prologue

The grimoires and their spirits have held a fascination for the magical student for all time. That spirits exist is not to be doubted, particularly after experiencing them; for then they will be beyond any doubt. The conjuration of spirits whilst a useful form of magic is demanding, and the arte does need a disciplined approach. A few years ago I and some others were involved in the conjuration of the Goetic spirit Seere, who amongst other things is diligent in attending to the will of the conjuror. Help was asked for by two people in resolving their housing problems as they were getting nowhere with their local Housing Authority.

The first individual had a major disability and it was quite clear that the authorities had no interest in their case. The second individual was much the same. After some thought and preparation a conjuration of the Goetic spirit Seere was performed to resolve the matter. At this point some folks may feel that we were taking a sledge hammer to crack a nut. Perhaps we were, but it still took some skilful handling. It was a familiar Goetic conjuration similar to the formula that is given in this work.

The atmosphere that can build up in acts of conjuration can be very intense, so much so that you can feel that anything is about to happen, often it does, and this was no exception. The long conjurations, the barbarous moaning words of power, half light and incense, the shapes and forms that can take place therein all lend their power to the working. Gazing into the shewstone the skryer said with some concern that the spirit had arrived and they were arising out of the shewstone. The skryer was alarmed that the spirit was angry for being disturbed, and had its face barely a foot away from the skryer's and was snarling at them! Making use of the formula given in this work for testing the spirits and to bring the situation under control the situation calmed down.

The skryer went on to describe the spirit as a man riding upon a horse. This was good as Seere will appear as such; more importantly I had not told the skryer which spirit was being conjured so that they had no prior knowledge of the traditional form of the spirit. Suddenly the shewstone darkened and great black clouds were rolling in the background. The spirit, whilst still astride the horse now had a great army behind them in long columns rising into the distance. At this point the spirit was instructed to present a member of their legion to come forth to perform the working that was required of them. A figure moved to the front dressed in deep blues bearing upon their chest the seal of the planet Jupiter which was coloured in silver.

To me this was of great significance as the astrology of the spirit's associations was of a Lunar and Jupiterian nature and the colours were therefore appropriate. The spirit is associated with the sign of Pisces (Jupiter) and the decan of Luna. Thus the symbol was true. The spirit agreed to resolve the problems and to influence the situation with the authorities to favour the two people in question, by a given time. The disabled individual had to vacate their privately rented home by the end of the week and was desperate as they were having to go into temporary accommodation. On the Thursday they were told that the bungalow that they had hoped to get was now allocated to somebody else, and they rang me in a distressed state.

Trying to calm the situation I said that I would get back onto the problem and I was sorry things hadn't worked as I had expected. Quietly I was furious with the spirit for what appeared to be a failure at such a time and started to think about the Goetic curses for rebellious spirits.

However for some reason I suggested that they should wait for the next day. Next morning they were back in touch, hysterical with joy, the people had gone into the property with their belongings and suddenly left! No reason was given and they left immediately, the housing association then offered the property to the disabled individual asking them if they could move in straight away; with their house packed it was no problem. The second individual's outcome was not quite so dramatic, whilst they had a pressing housing need they had applied for a particular property that was old and characterful, a rare type of property among housing association stock.

Several people had been offered the home and they had all walked into it and decided they did not like the atmosphere and left. This happened until the only person left with an interest was the person for whom the working had been done. Whilst *Goetia* conjuration is an effective part of the magical corpus, it will sometimes have you living life on the edge, as it can take you right to the wire before it resolves the situation. Although it is a powerful form of magic it is demanding too and if you can stick the pace you will find it highly effective.

CHAPTER ONE

Of Our Arte

Our Arte is a Mighty Arte and is not for the faint-hearted, nor is it for the fearful! It is demanding, disciplined and awe inspiring, and it can open the doors to *'A Perception of Creation,'* that is beyond the dreams of the common man; it can also smooth life's path too. This work approaches the arte of Goetic conjuration based upon experience and one that is successful. We must remember that our arte is what it says it is, an *'arte.'* However, we must also remember too, that we are not dealing with an exact science. Skill, will and determination are the keys to success, indeed as with all things in life. The seventy-two spirits of the *Goetia* are often deemed to be evil, yet their office when studied will show that they are like human nature, of a mixed good and evil disposition.

The spirits are bound to the conjuror's will by the use of the seventy-two angels who oppose them. The names of these angels are found in three verses from the book of *Exodus*, verses 19, 20, 21. These verses are written out in Hebrew in one line across the page, with the subsequent verses written out in a likewise manner below the first sentence. This will give when read downwards, seventy-two names consisting of three letters each. If each name is taken and either iah or el is added as an ending this will create the names of the seventy-two binding angels; who are also known as the Schemhamephorasch. These angels must be invoked as part of the conjuration to bind the spirit. This is done by the use of particular verses from the Psalms which are included as part of the rite.

On examination of the grimoire, influences from earlier works are apparent. For example, the *Heptameron* of Peter de Abano (1250-1316) can easily be seen as a source for the composer of the *Goetia* to have drawn upon. Some of the spirits can be found in a 15th century German manuscript which has been published by Richard Kieckhefer as *Forbidden Rites*.

Other grimoire scholars have drawn attention to the influence of earlier Greco-Egyptian works. Thomas Karlson also drew attention in *Qabalah, Qliphoth and Goetic Magic* to the fact that the numeration involved is based upon the Babylonian use of the number six, as our culture uses the number ten. Seventy-two spirits divisible by six, which are associated with the twelve signs of the Zodiac and the thirty-six decans thereof; again divisible by six. A persuasive thought that encourages the consideration that the grimoire's corpus is far older than has been previously considered. Thus those who are working within this system are clearly working with a magical tradition which is many hundreds of years old.

Do spirits appear when summoned? Invariably they do but do not always expect them to appear as the grimoires describe them. Nor do they need to appear visibly. You will know when they are present and if you are using a skryer and a shewstone they will find it easier to make contact because the earth plane is not their natural realm and thus they can find it difficult to manifest at this level without a lot of effort by the conjuror. It is easier for everyone to commune via the shewstone and this has been a traditional practice that many conjurors have used with good success. Some modern authorities have made it quite clear that a physical manifestation is not always necessary; (see Zalewski and DuQuette). I am also of this opinion unless you feel that physical manifestation is relevant to the working. My own preference is to use a shewstone and a competent skryer, and with this in my own practice of the arte I have had some excellent results from such workings.

Many will find the arte more accessible if they have had some magical experience and training and if they haven't I refer the reader to my earlier works, *Liber Noctis*, *Otz Chim* and *Ars Salomonis*, which they will find useful. Within some quarters of the magical community there is a debate as to whether the spirits are simply part of one's psyche or exist as entities in their own right, independent of the conjuror.

My own thoughts are that they exist at their own level and are real; however it is the conjuror that brings them into this world via their own psyche. The 20th century occultist Dion Fortune equated the subconscious mind correctly with the Kabbalistic realms of Yesod and it is through Yesod that energies, regardless of their origin, will ingress our levels of being. Thus the conjuror becomes a bridge between two worlds, and will be the means of ingress and egress. I have also given what I consider to be missing information that makes the working more likely to be successful. The spirits may only be summoned on a waxing moon and then only on the days that are even in number such as days 2-4-6-8-10-12-14 of the lunar cycle. By including the relevant astrological information, such as the incense, ruling King and direction, success, whilst not guaranteed, will be within reach. However this information is not that apparent when consulting the texts on *Goetia* which have so far been published and this work places this information firmly in the public domain; thus it is made accessible to the student of the magical artes. Also explored is secondary, but nonetheless important information, regarding the preparation and protocols that will be instrumental in granting success in one's experience of the arte of conjuration.

CHAPTER TWO

Of Those Spirits Both Darksome and Divine

Bael

Rank	King
Ruler	Goap
Archangel	Mikael
Sign	♈ 0°-4°
Direction	East
Incense	Frankincense and pepper
Sigil colour	Red and gold
Metal	Gold
Time to be conjured	Between 9am-noon, 3pm-sunset

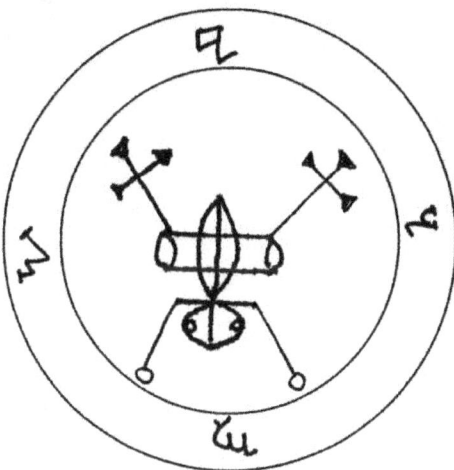

The first spirit is a king who rules in the east. He grants invisibility and rules over 60 legions of spirits and appears in diverse shapes. Sometimes like a cat or toad and sometimes as a man, or even all three shapes at once. He speaks hoarsely and his seal must be worn as a lamen before him by those who would call him forth, or he will not obey.

Binding Angel: Vehuiah

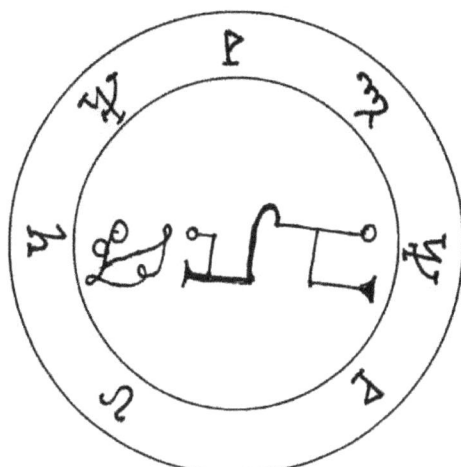

Vehuiah helps to expand consciousness and grants enlightenment. This angel dominates the sciences and influences the shrewd.

Angelic conjuration:

> *'Tu Domini Susceptor,*
> *Meus es Gloria Mea et Exaltans Caput Meum.'*

> *'Thou, O Lord Art My Guardian & Exalted Head.'*

Psalm 3:5

Agares

Rank	Duke
Ruler	Goap
Archangel	Mikael
Sign	♈ 5°-9°
Direction	East
Incense	Rose and pepper
Sigil colour	Red and gold
Metal	Copper
Time to be conjured	Between sunrise and noon in clear weather

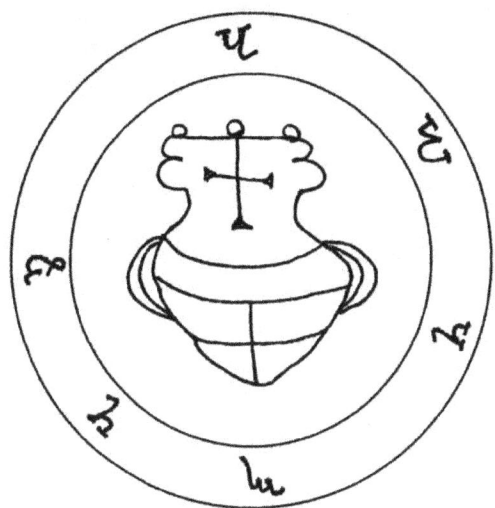

Agares is the second spirit and is a duke who is associated with the 5°-9° of Aries. Thus he is associated with the east. He appears in the form of an old man riding upon a crocodile. He carries a goshawk upon his fist, and is mild in appearance. He brings back runaways and makes those who stand still to run. He teaches all languages and has the power to destroy dignities both spiritual and temporal. He causes earthquakes and was of the order of virtues. He governs 31 legions of spirits.

Binding Angel: Ieliel

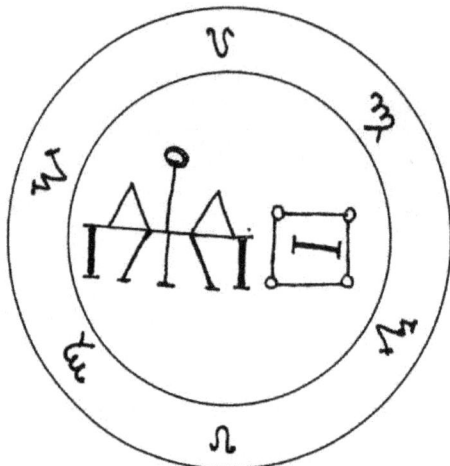

Ieliel helps to repress unjust revolts and aids in conjugal peace. This angel dominates kings and princes and influences generations.

Angelic conjuration:

'Et tu Domine ne Elongaveris Auxiliam Tuum A me, ad Defensionem Meum Conspice.'

'Do not remove thy help from me O Lord and look to my defense.'

Psalm 21:20

Vassago

Rank	Prince
Ruler	Goap
Archangel	Mikael
Sign	♈ 10°-14°
Incense	Cedar and frankincense
Direction	East
Sigil colour	Blue and gold
Metal	Tin
Time of conjuration	Anytime

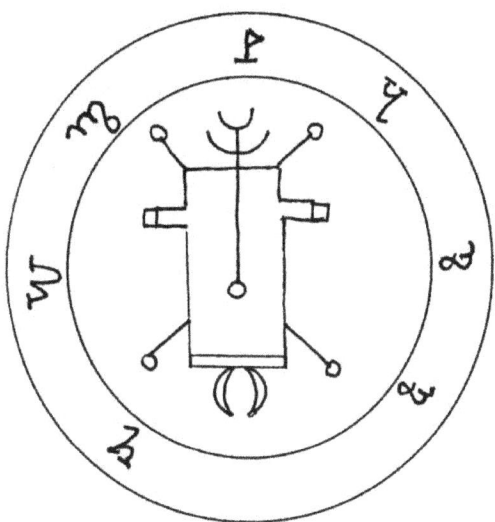

The third spirit is a mighty being of the same nature as Agares. He is of a good nature and his office is to declare things past and to come. Also to discover all things hid or lost. He governs 26 legions of spirits.

Binding Angel: Sitael

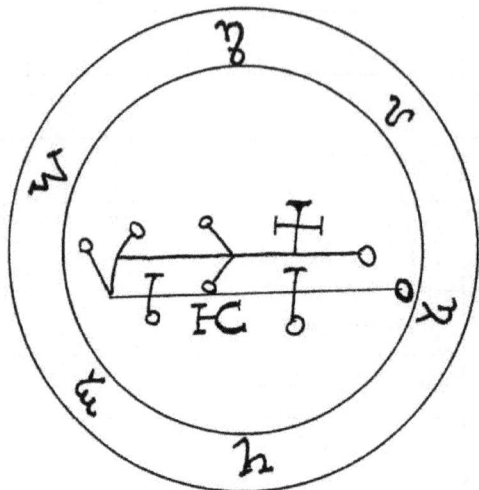

This angel will protect against adversity and calamity: Dominates magnanimity and nobility. Influences all those who are lovers of truth.

Angelic conjuration:

'Dicam Domino Susceptor Meus es Tu, Et refugium Meum Deus Meus Sperabo in Sum.'

'I shall say to the Lord, Thou art my guardian, My God is my refuge & I shall hope in him.'

Psalm 90:2

Samigina

Rank	Marquis
Ruler	Goap
Archangel	Mikael
Sign	♈ 15°-19°
Direction	East
Incense	Frankincense and jasmine
Sigil colour	Gold and purple
Metal	Silver
Time of conjuration	Between 3pm and sunrise next day

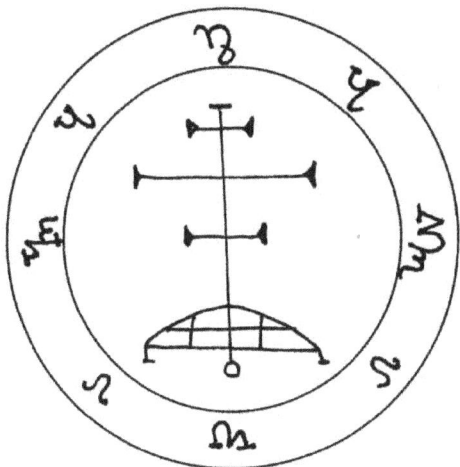

This spirit is also known as Gamigin and is a great Marquis. He appears in the form of a little horse or ass and then into human shape. He will change appearance at the request of the conjuror and speaks with a hoarse voice. He rules over 30 legions of spirits and teaches all liberal sciences and gives accounts of dead souls that died in sin.

Binding Angel: Elemiah

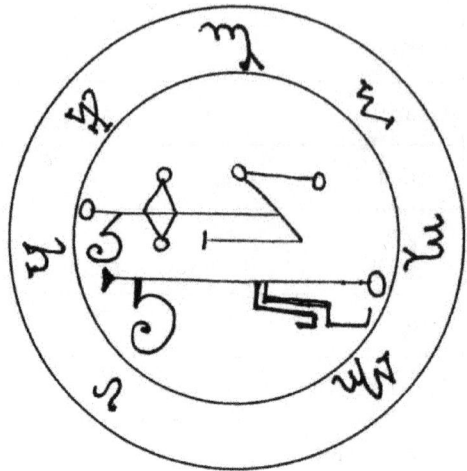

This angel will help against spiritual torment, they will also reveal traitors. They dominate sea voyages and also influence discoveries.

Angelic conjuration:

'*Convertere Domino et Eripe Animam Meum Salvum Me Fac Propter Misericordium Tuam.*'

'*Turn O Lord & Deliver My Soul And Save Me for Thy Mercies' Sake.*'

Psalm 6:4

Marbas

Rank	President
Ruler	Goap
Archangel	Mikael
Sign	♈ 20°-24°
Direction	East
Incense	Cedar and lavender
Sigil colour	Blue and orange
Metal	Mercury
Time of conjuration	Anytime except at twilight at night unless the King has been invoked first to assist

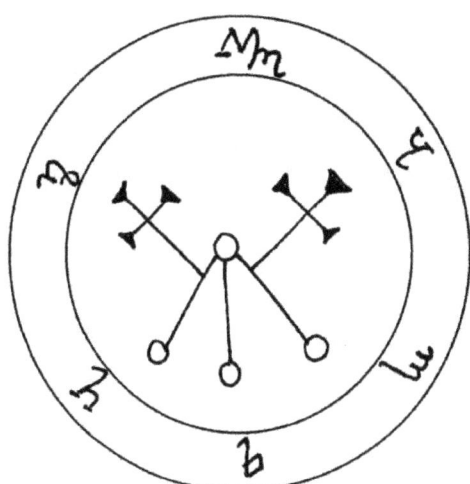

This spirit is a great President and will first appear as a great lion, but will adopt human shape if commanded by the conjuror. He will answer truly of all things hidden or secret. He can cause disease and cure them. He will also grant wisdom and knowledge in mechanical arts.

He can also change men into other shapes and he governs 36 legions of spirits.

Binding Angel: Mehasiah

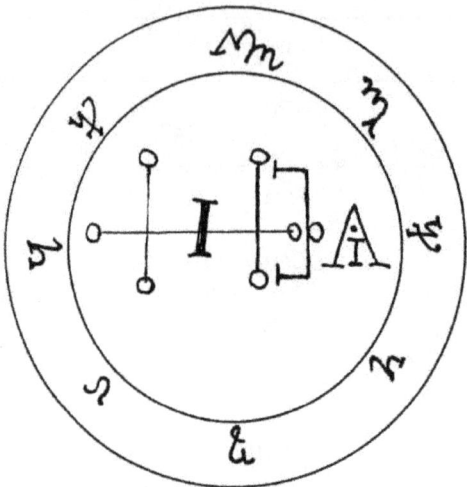

This angel will help to live in peace and they dominate all occult, magic and theology. They will also influence learning.

Angelic conjuration:

> 'Ex qui sivi Dominum et exaudivit me et ex omnibus tribulationibus eripuit me.'

> 'I called upon the Lord & he heard me and delivered me from my tribulations.'

Psalm 33:4

Valefor

Rank	Duke
Ruler	Goap
Archangel	Mikael
Sign	♈ 25-30°
Direction	East
Incense	Cedar and rose
Sigil colour	Blue and green
Metal	Copper
Time of conjuration	Sunrise till noon in clear weather

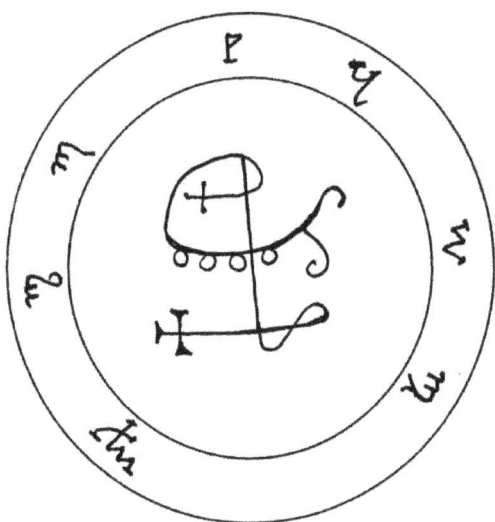

The sixth spirit is Valefor. He is a mighty duke and will appear in the shape of a lion, with an asses' head bellowing. He is a good familiar but will tempt the conjuror to steal.

He governs 10 legions of spirits.

Binding Angel: Lelahel

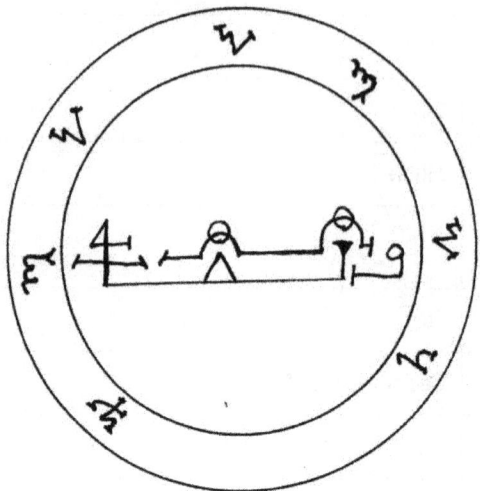

Serves to acquire *'light.'* Will help to cure contagious diseases and dominates love, fame and fortune. Also influences the sciences.

Angelic conjuration:

'Psallite Domino habitat in Sion Annunciate inter gentes studia eius.'

'Let him who lives in Zion sing unto the Lord And proclaim his goodwill among the peoples.'

Psalm 9:11

Amon

Rank	Marquis
Ruler	Ziminiar
Archangel	Auriel
Sign	♉ 1°-5°
Direction	South
Incense	Jasmine and rose
Sigil colour	Green and purple
Metal	Silver
Time of conjuration	From 3pm until sunrise the next day

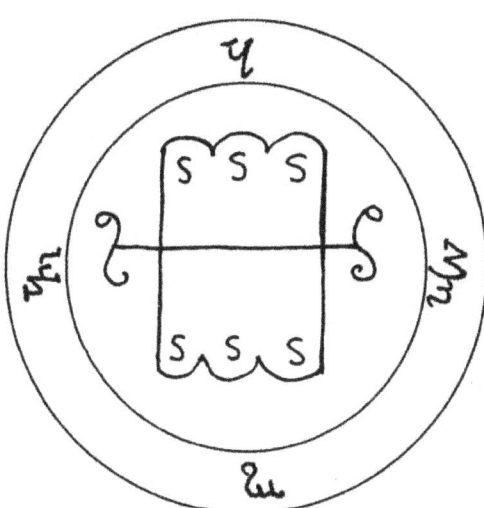

    The seventh spirit is a great marquis, who is both powerful and strong. He will at first appear as a wolf with a serpent's tail. He will pour forth fire from his mouth. Sometimes he will appear as a raven with dogs' teeth. He will tell of all things past, present and to come. He will promote love and reconciliation. He governs 40 legions of spirits.

Binding Angel: Achiah

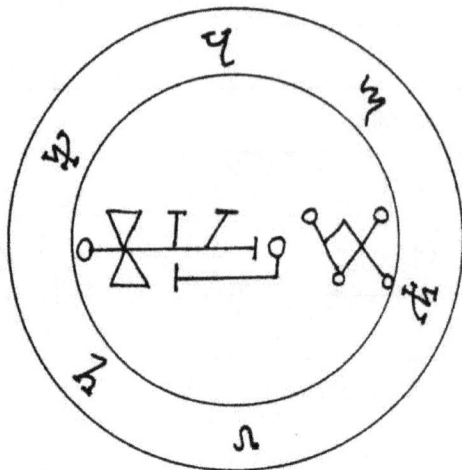

This angel helps to discover secrets; they also dominate patience and temperance. He will also promote light and industry.

Angelic conjuration:

> 'Miserator et misericors Dominus Longanimus et multum misericors.'

> 'The Lord is merciful & compassionate Long-suffering and of great goodness.'

Psalm 103:8

Barbatos

Rank	Duke
Ruler	Ziminiar
Archangel	Auriel
Sign	♉ 5°-9°
Direction	South
Incense	Rose
Sigil colour	Green
Metal	Copper
Time of conjuration	Sunrise to noon

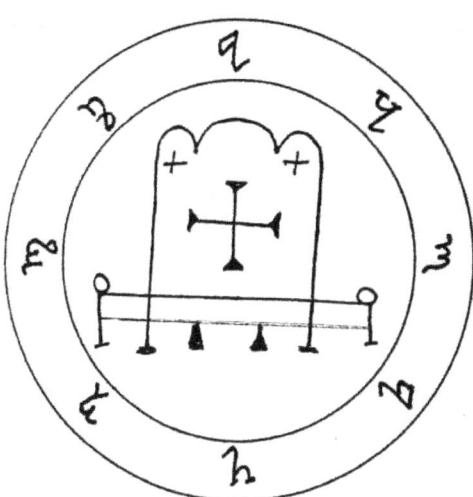

Barbatos is a great duke and appears when the sun is in Sagittarius, with four noble kings and their companies of great troops. He grants understanding of the singing of birds and the voices of all creatures, such as the barking of dogs. He will find hidden treasures and break the enchantments that hide them. He is of the order of virtues of which some part he retains. He also knows of all things that are past present and to come. He will reconcile friends and those who are in power. And he rules over 30 legions of spirits.

Binding Angel: Kahetel

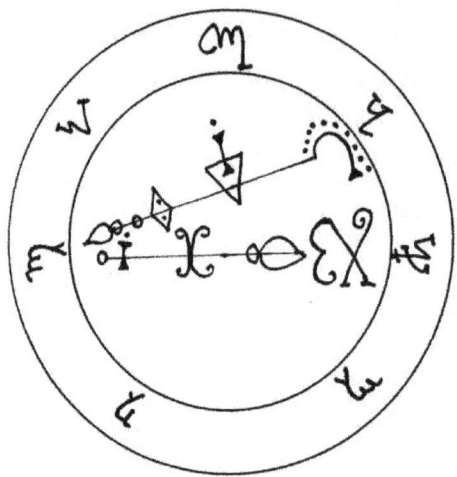

He serves to obtain blessing and protection against evil spirits. Dominates agricultural produce. Influences the hunt.

Angelic conjuration:

'*Venite Adoremus et Procedamus Ante Dominum Qui Fecit nos.*'

'*O Come Let Us Adore and Fall Down Before God Who Bore Us.*'

Psalm 95:6

Paimon

Rank	King
Ruler	Ziminiar
Archangel	Auriel
Sign	♉ 10°-14°
Direction	South
Incense	Lavender and frankincense
Sigil colour	Gold and orange
Metal	Gold
Time of conjuration	9am – noon & 3pm till sunset

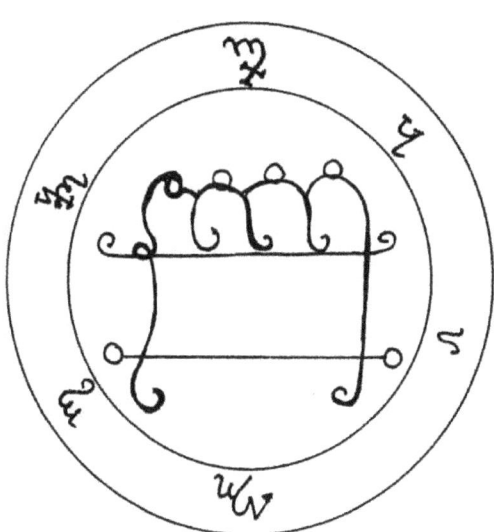

Paimon is a Great King and very obedient to Lucifer; he appears as a man wearing a crown and sits upon a dromedary. There goes before him a large host of spirits with cymbals, trumpets and other musical instruments. He has a loud voice and will roar at his coming. His speech is not easy to understand unless he is compelled to speak clearly. He teaches all artes and sciences, he also teaches all secret things.

He will reveal what the earth is and what holds it up in the waters. Also what the wind is and where it is and anything that you desire to know. He gives dignity and confirms it. Binds men to the magician's will. He gives good familiars that teach all arte. He is observed towards the west and is of the order of Dominions. He has 200 legions and must have offerings.

Binding Angel: Aiel

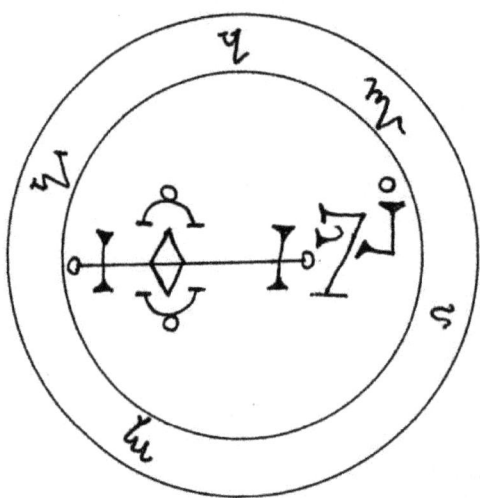

Helps keeps promises and obtains the friendship of the great. Dominates good faith: Influences sincerity & faith.

Angelic conjuration:

'*Reminiscere miserationum tuarum Domine Et miserationum tuarum quae a saeculo sunt.*'

Remember thy mercies O Lord and thy mercies which have been forever.'

Psalm 25:6

Buer

Rank	President
Ruler	Ziminiar
Archangel	Auriel
Sign	♉ 15°-19°
Direction	South
Incense	Lavender
Sigil colour	Orange
Metal	Mercury
Time of conjuration	Anytime except twilight at night unless the king has been invoked first

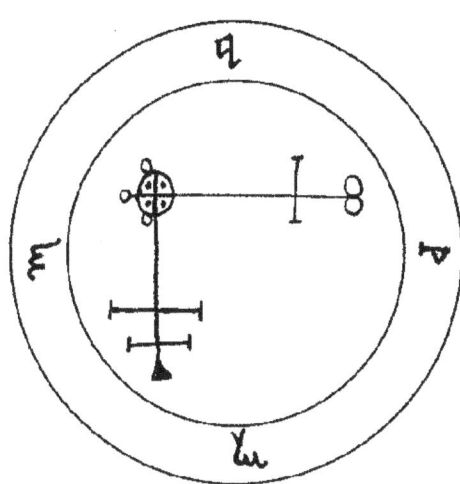

Buer will appear when the sun is in Sagittarius. He teaches philosophy, both moral and natural; also the arte of logic. He will also instruct in the virtues of herbs and plants that will heal. He grants good familiars and governs 50 legions of spirits.

Binding Angel: Aladiah

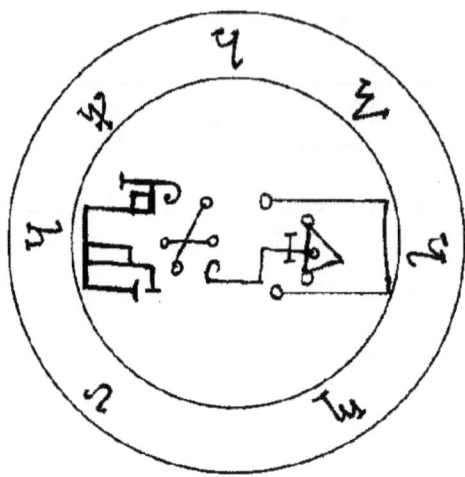

Helps to hide secrets. Dominates plague and rabies. Influences healing.

Angelic conjuration:

'Fiat misericordia tua super nos quemadmodum speravimus in te.'

'Perform thy mercies upon us for we have hoped in thee.'

Psalm 33:22

Gusion

Rank	Duke
Ruler	Ziminiar
Archangel	Auriel
Sign	♉ 20°-24°
Direction	South
Incense	Myrrh and rose
Metal	Copper
Sigil colour	Black and green
Time of conjuration	Sunrise until noon in clear weather

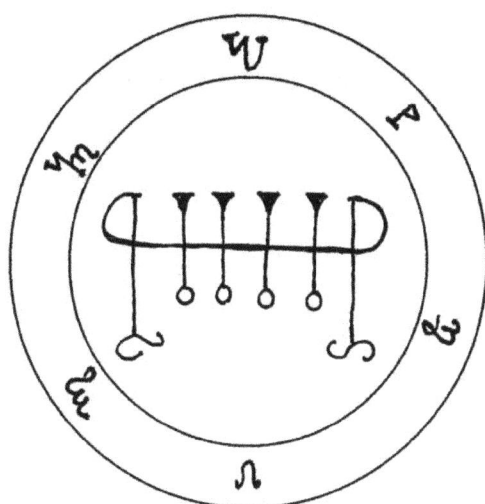

The eleventh spirit is a great and strong duke who appears in the form of a Xenophilus. He will teach of all things that are past, present and to come. He shows the meaning of all questions and will reconcile friend and foe. He grants honours and dignities and rules over 40 legions of spirits.

Binding Angel: Lauviah

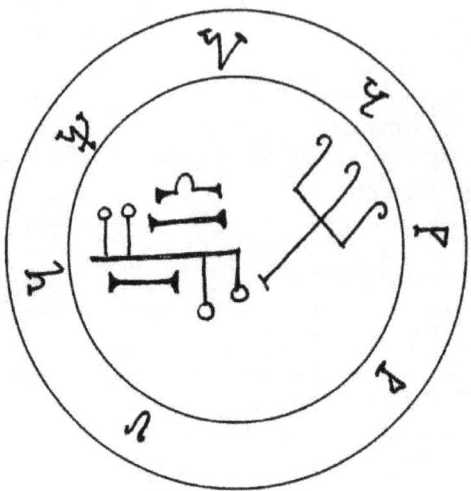

Protects against lightning. Also will help in granting victory. Also dominates fame and influences the learned.

Angelic conjuration:

'Vivit Dominus et benedictus Deus meus et exaltetur Deus salutis meae.'

'The Lord liveth blessed is my God and let the God of my salvation be exalted.'

Psalm 18:47

Sitri

Rank	Prince
Ruler	Ziminiar
Archangel	Auriel
Sign	♉ 25°-29°
Direction	South
Incense	Myrrh and cedar
Sigil colour	Grey and blue
Metal	Tin
Time of conjuration	Any hour of the day

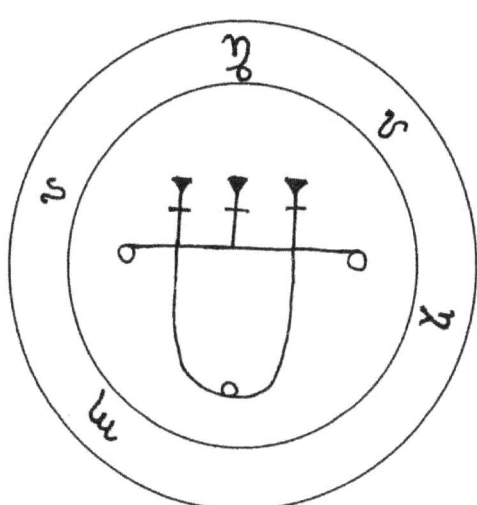

The twelfth spirit is Sitri and he is a great prince. He appears at first with a leopard's head and with the wings of a griffin. He will assume human shape when commanded to do so and that will be very beautiful. He grants the love of both men and women. He will also cause them to show themselves naked. He governs 60 legions of spirits.

Binding Angel: Hahiah

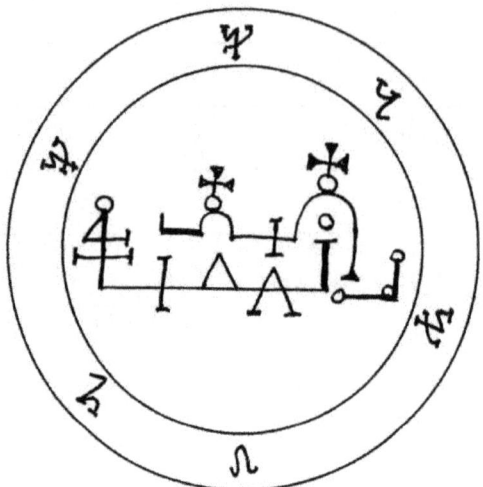

Protects against adversity and helps those in need. Dominates dreams and influences wise and spiritual people.

Angelic conjuration:

> 'Ut quid, Domine, recessisti longe despicis In opportunitatibus in tribulatione.'

> 'Why hast thou departed O Lord so long from us perishing in the times of tribulation.'

Psalm 10:1

Beleth

Rank	King
Ruler	Amaymon
Archangel	Raphael
Sign	♊ 0°-4°
Direction	West
Incense	Lavender and frankincense
Sigil colour	Gold and orange
Metal	Gold
Time of conjuration	9am-noon or 3pm-sunset

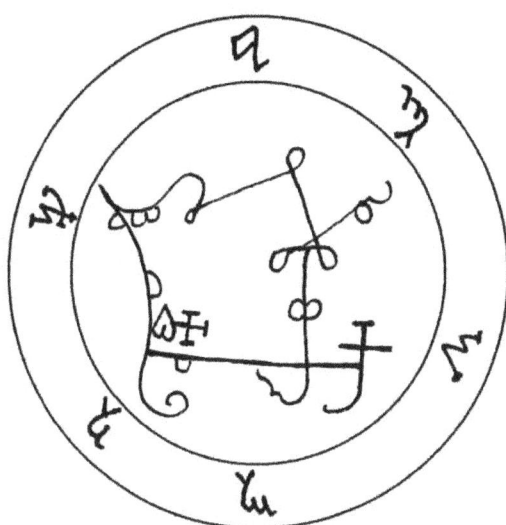

The thirteenth spirit of our arte is called Beleth and he is a mighty and terrible king. He rides upon a pale horse with trumpets and other kinds of musical instruments playing before him. He is very furious at his first appearance. The conjuror will need to have a wand of hazel, with which they must strike the south and eastern quarters. After which the conjuror will need to command the spirit into the triangle of arte which will be outside the circle and in the east.

As he is a great king he must be treated accordingly and the conjuror will need to wear the silver ring on their middle left finger, this will need to be held near the face. Beleth will cause the love of both men and women. He is of the Order of Powers and governs 85 legions of spirits.

Binding Angel: Yezalel

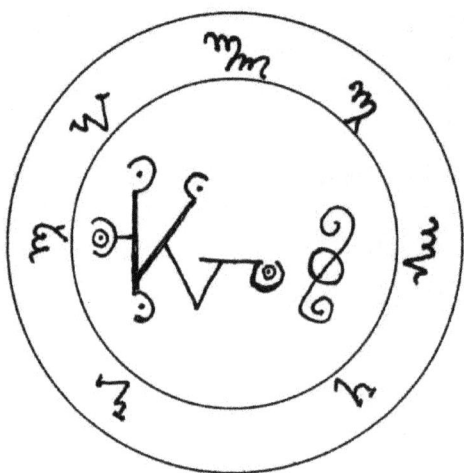

Helps reconciliation and conjugal faithfulness. Dominates friendships and affability. He will also influence memory and shrewdness.

Angelic conjuration:

'Jubilate Domino omnis terra cantate et exultate, et psallite.'

'Rejoice in the Lord all ye lands sing exult and play upon a stringed instrument.'

Psalm 97:6

Leraje

Rank	Marquis
Ruler	Amaymon
Archangel	Raphael
Sign	♊ 5°-9°
Direction	West
Incense	Lavender and jasmine
Metal	Silver
Sigil colour	Orange and purple
Time of conjuration	3pm- sunrise

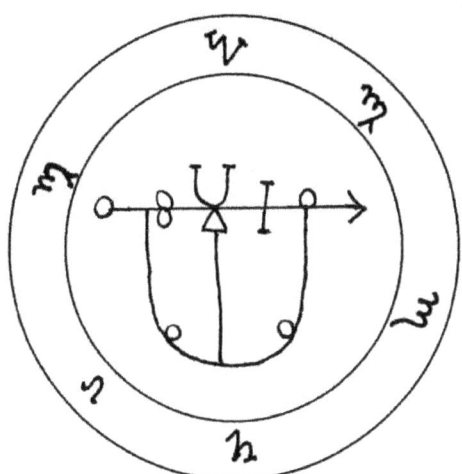

Leraje is a great marquis and shows himself in the likeness of an archer who is clad in green. He carries bow and quiver, he causes battles and contests. He also makes wounds that are inflicted by arrows slow to heal, and he governs 30 legions.

Binding Angel: Mebahel

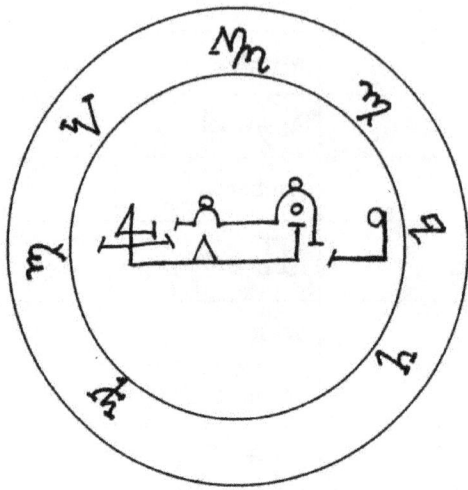

The angel will protect against the usurping of the fortunes of others. He dominates justice and will protect the truth.

Angelic conjuration:

> *'Et factus est Dominus refugium pauperi adjutor in opportunitatibus in tribulatione.'*
>
> *'The Lord also will be a refuge for the oppressed, a refuge in times of trouble.'*

Psalm 9:9

Eligos

Rank	Duke
Ruler	Amaymon
Archangel	Raphael
Sign	♊ 10°-14°
Direction	West
Incense	Rose and red sandalwood
Metal	Copper.
Sigil colour	Green
Time of conjuration	Sunrise to noon in clear weather

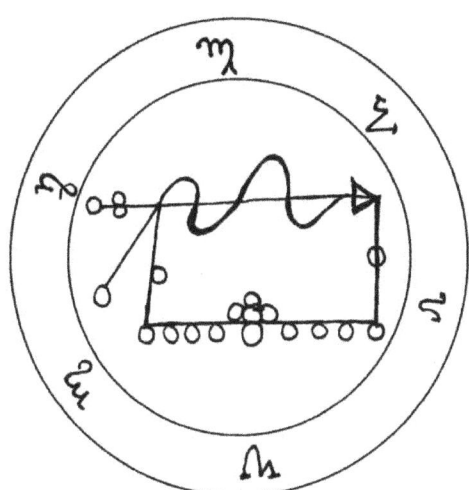

The fifteenth spirit Eligos is a great duke who appears in the form of a goodly knight carrying a lance and ensign and also a serpent. He will discover all things that be hidden and will show things to come. He will tell of wars and how soldiers will meet. He causeth the love of lords and great persons. He governs 60 legions of spirits.

Binding Angel: Haril

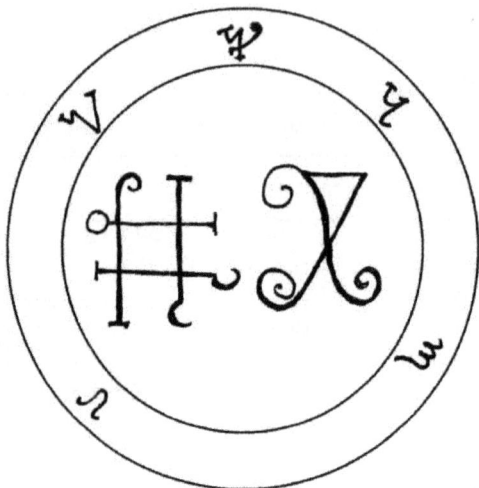

Serves against the ungodly and defeatist. This angel dominates the sciences and arts; they also influence discoveries and all new methods.

Angelic conjuration:

> 'Et factus est mihi Dominus in refugium et Deus meus in adjutorium spei meae'

> 'The Lord is a refuge for me and my God the help of my hope.'

Psalm 93:22

Zepar

Rank	Duke
Ruler	Amaymon
Archangel	Raphael
Sign	♊ 15°- 19°
Direction	West
Incense	Rose
Sigil colour	Green
Metal	Copper
Time of conjuration	Sunrise until noon time in clear weather

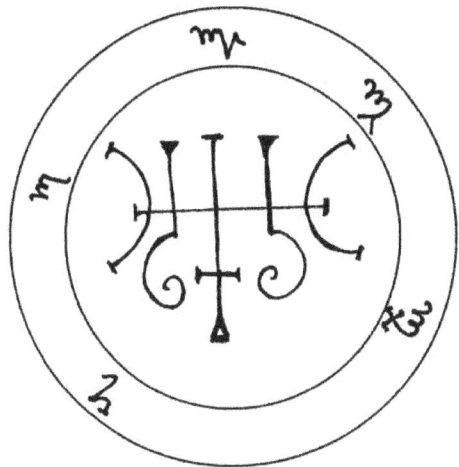

The sixteenth spirit is a duke called Zepar: he is a great duke and appears in red armour. His office is to cause women to love men and to bring them together in love. He will also make them barren. He governeth 26 legions of inferior spirits and his seal is thus which he obeyeth when it is shown unto him.

Binding Angel: Hakamiah

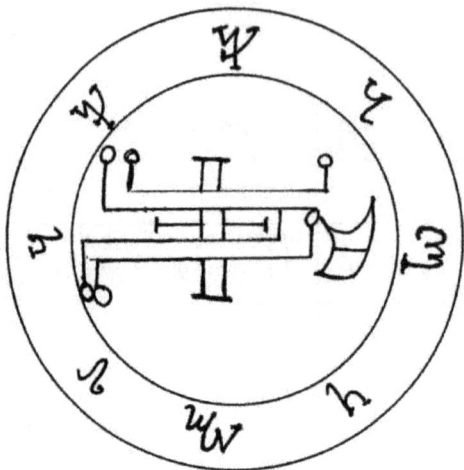

Helps against the plots of traitors and those who will do you ill. This angel will help grant victory over enemies. Dominates military matters and influences frankness.

Angelic conjuration:

'*Domine Deus salutis meae in die clamavi et nocte coram te.*'

'O Lord God of my salvation by day have I called to thee and sought thy presence by night.'

Psalm 87:1

Botis

Rank	President & earl
Ruler	Amaymon
Archangel	Raphael
Sign	♊ 20°-24°
Incense	Lavender and myrrh
Metal	Mercury
Sigil colour	Green and purple
Time of conjuration	Anytime except twilight, if invocated first

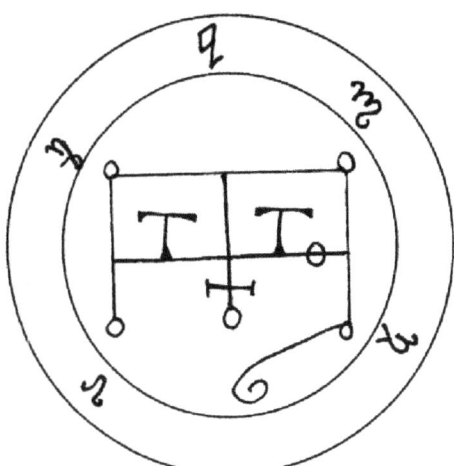

Botis is the seventeenth spirit and he will appear as an ugly viper at first. At the command of the conjuror he will take on human form, but with great teeth and with horns. He carries a bright and sharp sword in his hand and he will tell of all things past and to come. He reconciles friends and foes and he rules over 68 legions of spirits.

Binding Angel: Leviah

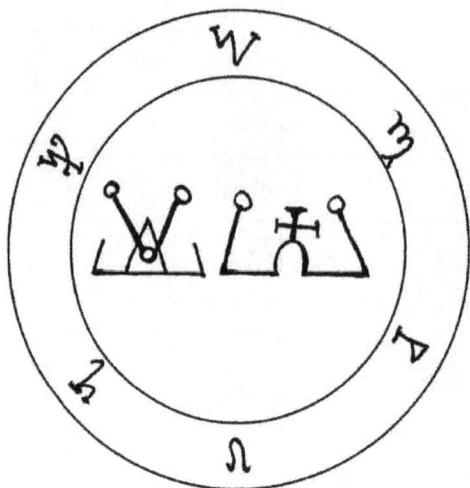

Helps against sadness and dominates the higher sciences. Also influences musicians and poets.

Angelic conjuration:

'Domine Dominus noster quam admirabile est nomen tuum in universa terra.'

'O Lord our Lord how wonderful is thy name in all the world.'

Psalm 8:1

Bathin

Rank	Duke
Ruler	Amaymon
Archangel	Raphael
Sign	♊ 25°-29°
Direction	West
Incense	Rose and myrrh
Sigil colour	Green and black
Metal	Copper
Time of conjuration	Sunrise until noon in clear weather

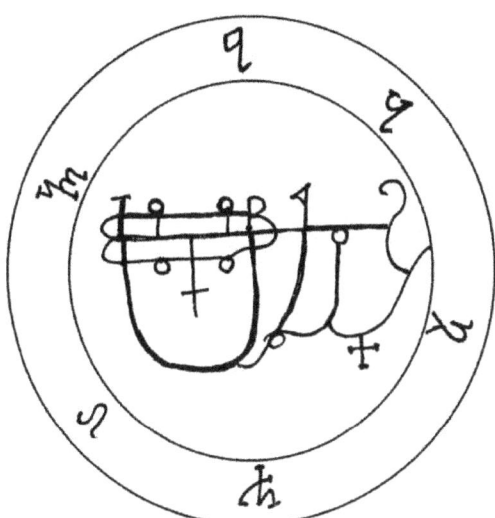

The eighteenth spirit is Bathin and he is a mighty and strong duke. He appears like a strong man with a tail of a serpent and sits upon a pale horse. He knows the virtue of herb and stone, he can also transport men suddenly from one country to another; he rules over 30 legions of spirits.

Binding Angel: Caliel

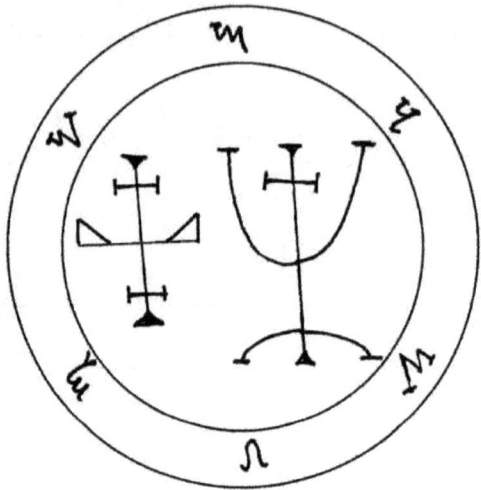

Serves to reveal the truth, also aids the triumph of the innocent. Will dominate the outcome of all trials and will influence witnesses.

Angelic conjuration:

'Iudica me Domine secundum Misericordiam et Iustitiam tuam Domine Deus meus et non supergaudeat mihi.'

'Judge me O Lord according to thy loving kindness and let them not be joyful over me, O Lord.'

Psalm 35:24

Sallos

Rank	Duke
Ruler	Corson
Archangel	Gabriel
Sign	♋ 0°-4°
Direction	North
Incense	Rose and jasmine
Sigil colour	Green and purple
Metal	Copper
Time of conjuration	Sunrise until noon in clear weather

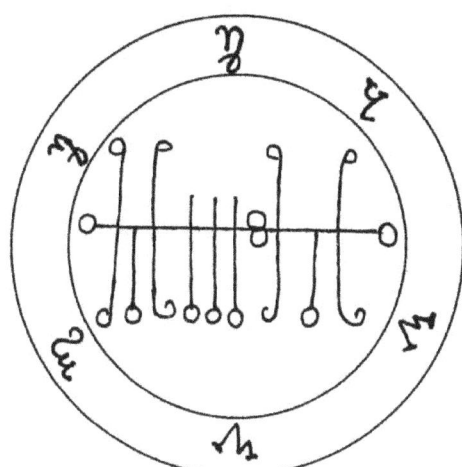

Sallos is the nineteenth spirit and is a great and mighty spirit, who appears as a gallant soldier riding on a crocodile, with a ducal crown upon his head. He appears peaceably. He causes the love of women to men and vice versa. He governs 30 legions of spirits.

Binding Angel: Leuviah

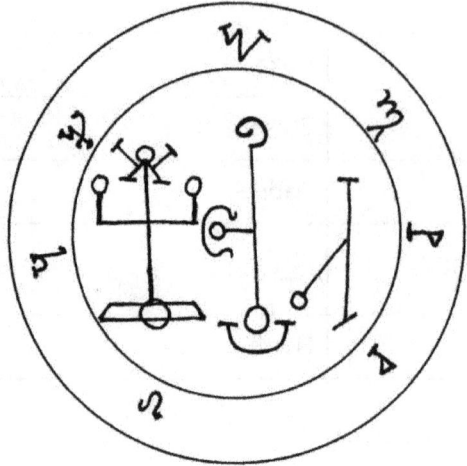

Protects and helps in obtaining grace, influences the memory, joviality and intelligence.

Angelic conjuration:

'Expectans expectavi Dominum et intendit mihi.'

'I waited in hope for the Lord and he turned to me.'

Psalm 39:1

Purson

Rank	King
Ruler	Corson
Archangel	Gabriel
Sign	♋ 5°-9°
Direction	North
Incense	Frankincense and jasmine
Sigil colour	Gold and purple
Metal	Gold
Time of conjuration	9am-noon and 3pm-sunset

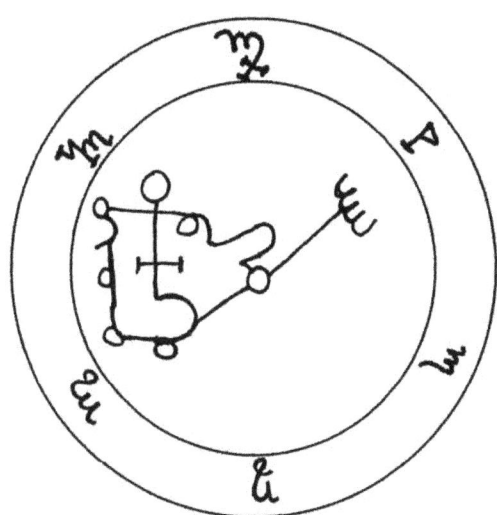

The twentieth spirit is Purson who is a great King. His appearance is comely like a man with a lion's face. He carries a viper in his hand and he rides a bear. Going before him are many trumpets sounding. He knows of all things which are hidden, and can also discover treasure. He tells of all things of the past, present and to come. He can take on human appearance; he will answer truthfully of all earthly things both secret and divine.

He will also talk of the creation of the world. He gives good familiars too. Under his governance are 20 legions of spirits who are partly of the order of the thrones. He is obedient unto his seal.

Binding Angel: Pahaliah

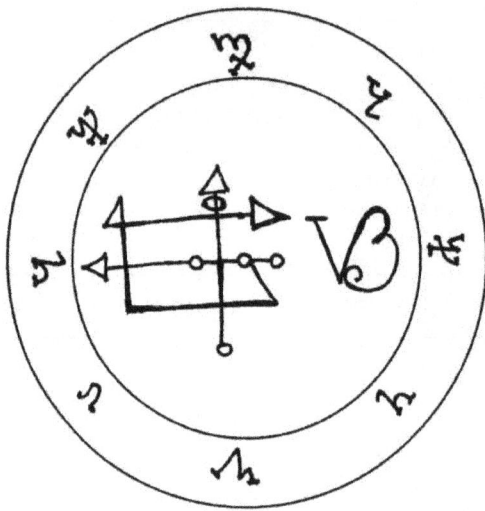

Helps conversions, dominates theology and religion. Will also influence chastity and morals.

Angelic conjuration:

'Et nomen Domini invocabo O Domini Libera animam meum.'

'I shall call upon the name of the Lord O Lord free my soul.'

Psalm 119:2

Marax

Rank	Prince and Earl
Ruler	Corson
Archangel	Gabriel
Sign	♋ 10°-14°
Direction	North
Incense	Dragon's blood and pepper
Sigil colour	Red
Metal	Tin
Time of conjuration	Any hour of the day

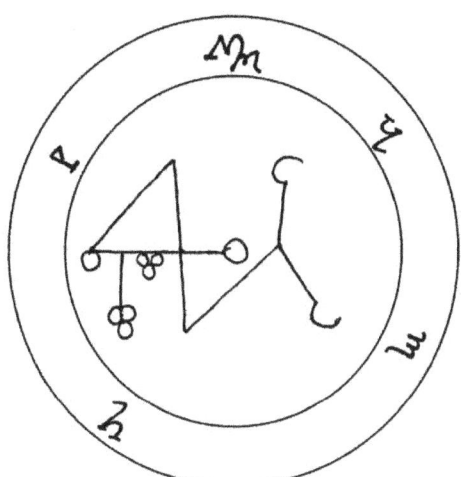

Marax is the twenty-first spirit and is a great earl and president. He will appear like a great bull with a man's face. His office is to make very knowing in astronomy and all liberal sciences. Also he can give good familiars. He knows the virtue of herb and stone. He governs 30 legions of spirits.

Binding Angel: Nelekael

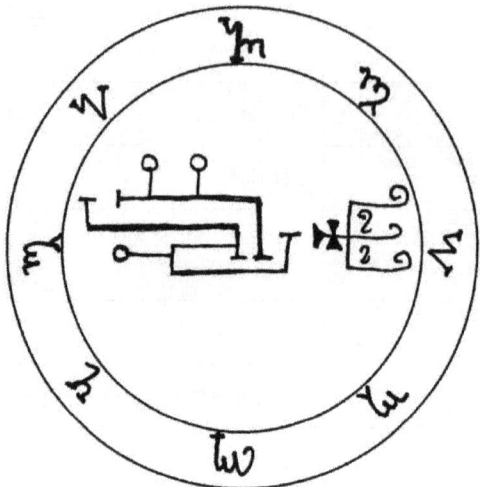

Protects against unfavourable spirits and slander. Dominates mathematics and geometry.

Angelic conjuration:

'Ego autem in te speravi Domine Dixi Deus meus es tu.'

'In thee also have I hoped O Lord and said thou art my God.'
Psalm 30:18

Ipos

Rank	Prince
Ruler	Corson
Archangel	Gabriel
Sign	♋ 15°-19°
Direction	North
Incense	Cedar and dragon's blood
Sigil colour	Blue and red
Metal	Tin
Time of conjuration	Any hour of the day

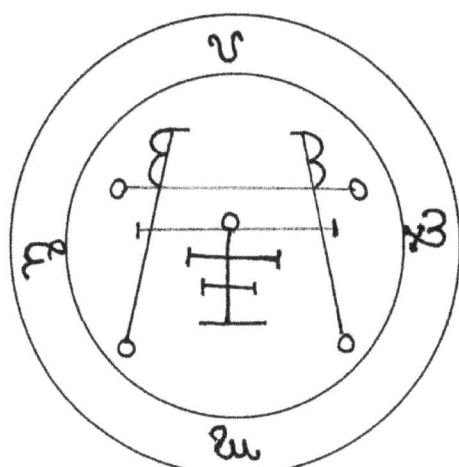

The spirit Ipos is an earl and also a mighty prince who appears in the form of a mighty angel with a lion's head, with webbed feet and a hare's tail. He knows of all things past, present and to come. He makes men witty and bold and governs 36 legions of spirits.

Binding Angel: Yeiael

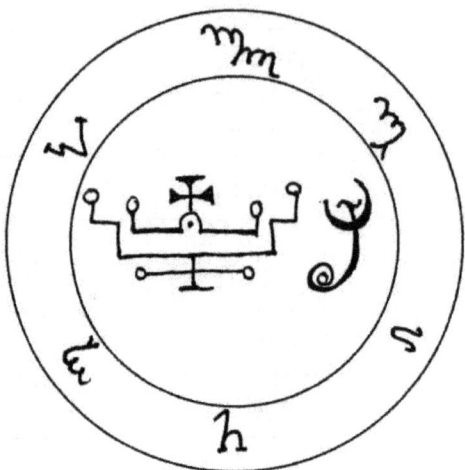

Protects against storms and ship wrecks, and dominates business fortunes. Will also influence business trips.

Angelic invocation:

'Dominus custodit te, Dominus protectio tua super manum dextram tuam.'

'The Lord keep thee, The Lord be thy protection on thy right hand.'
Psalm 120:5

Aim

Rank	Duke
Ruler	Corson
Archangel	Gabriel
Sign	♋ 20°-24°
Direction	North
Incense	Rose and cedar
Sigil colour	Green and blue
Metal	Copper
Time of conjuration	Sunrise until noon in clear weather.

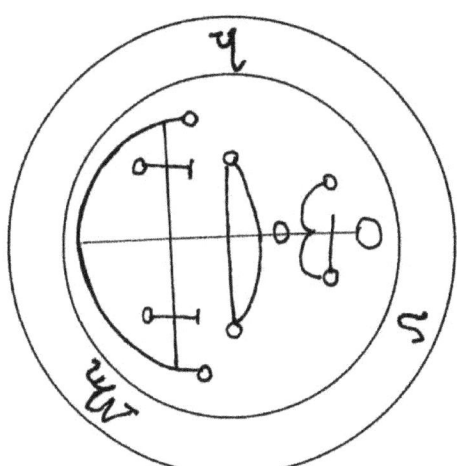

The twenty-third spirit is Aim and he is a great and strong duke, who appears in the form of a comely man with three heads. The first like a serpent, the second like a man with two stars upon his forehead and the third like a calf. He rideth upon a viper carrying a fire brand in each hand, wherewith he sets cities, castles and great palaces on fire. He maketh people witty in all manner of ways and also gives true answers unto private matters. He governs 26 legions of inferior spirits.

Binding Angel: Melanel

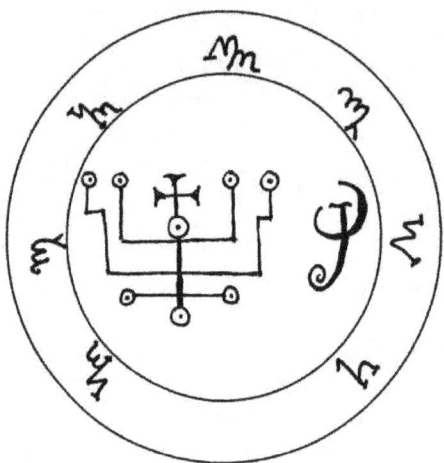

Protects against weapons and the perils of travel, also dominates medical herbs and water.

Angelic conjuration:

> 'Dominus custodiat introitum tuum
> et exitum tuum ex nunc et usque in seculum.'

> 'The Lord keep thine incoming and thine outgoing from this time forth for evermore.'

Psalm 120:8

Naberius

Rank	Marquis
Ruler	Corson
Archangel	Gabriel
Sign	♋ 25°-29°
Direction	North
Incense	Jasmine and cedar
Sigil colour	Purple and blue
Metal	Silver
Time of conjuration	3pm till sunrise

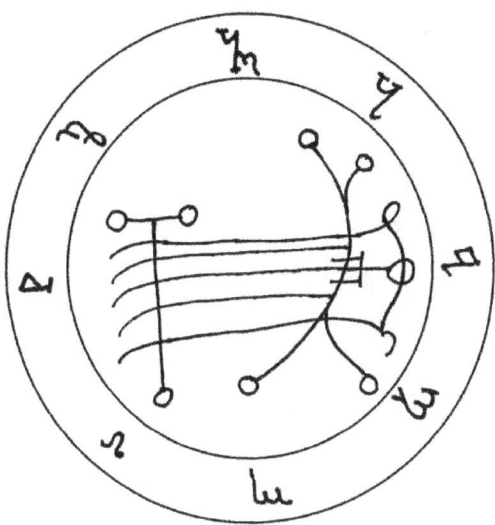

Naberius is the twenty-fourth spirit and is a most valiant marquis and appears in the form of a black crane who speaks with a hoarse voice. He makes men cunning in all arts and sciences, particularly rhetoric. He will restore lost dignity and honour. He governs 19 legions of spirits.

Binding Angel: Hahuiah

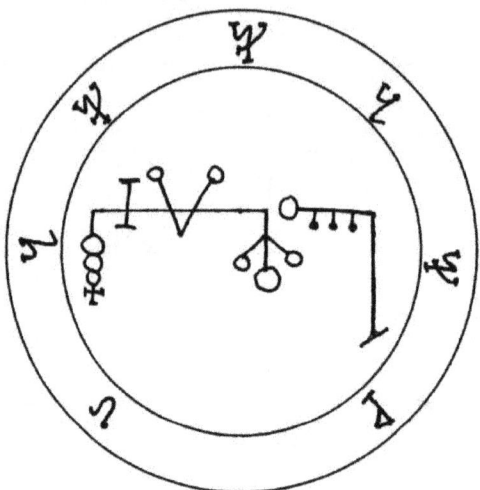

Serves to obtain grace. Dominates the exiled and protects against thieves and murderers.

Angelic conjuration:

> 'Beneplacitum est Domino super timentes eum.
> Et in iis qui sperant super misericordiam eius.'

> 'The Lord is well pleased with those that fear him and hope upon his mercy.'

Psalm 32:18

Glasya-Labolas

Rank	President
Ruler	Goap
Archangel	Mikael
Sign	♌ 0°-4°
Direction	East
Incense	Frankincense and lavender
Sigil colour	Gold and orange
Metal	Mercury
Time of conjuration	Any time except twilight and if at night the king must be invoked first.

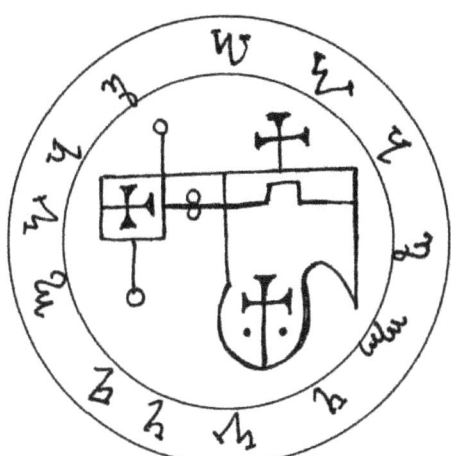

Glasya-Labolas is the twenty-fifth spirit and is a mighty president and earl. He will appear as a dog with wings, like a gryphon and will teach of all artes and science. But he can also create blood and manslaughter. He will teach of all things past, present and to come. He will also cause the love of friend and foe, and will also make the conjuror invisible. He commands 30 legions.

Binding Angel: Nith-Haiah

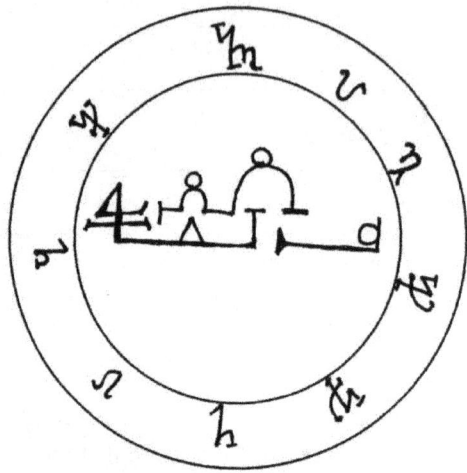

Serves to obtain wisdom and have dream revelations. Dominates the occult sciences and the wise.

Angelic conjuration:

'Confitebor tibi Domine in tote corde meo narrabo omnia mirabilia tua.'

'I shall acknowledge thee O Lord with all my heart and shall tell forth all thy wonders.'

Psalm 9:2

Bune

Rank	Duke
Ruler	Goap
Archangel	Mikael
Sign	♌ 5°-9°
Direction	East
Incense	Frankincense and rose
Sigil colour	Gold and green
Metal	Copper
Time of conjuration	Sunrise until noon in clear weather

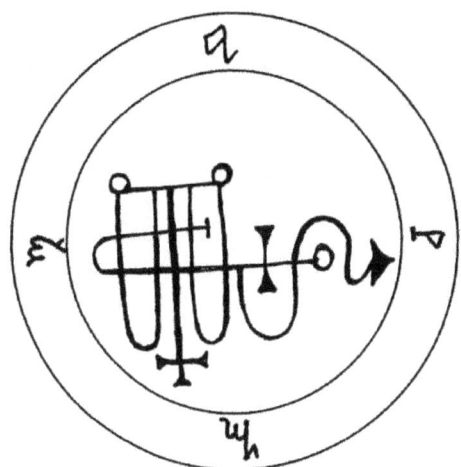

The twenty-sixth spirit is called Bune and he is a great and strong Duke who will appear as a dragon with three heads, one like a dog, one like a gryphon and one like a man. He will speak with a high and comely voice. He changes the places of the dead and causes those spirits under him to gather upon graves. He will grant riches unto man and will make him wise and eloquent. He gives true answers to demands and he governeth 30 legions of spirits.

Binding Angel: Haaih

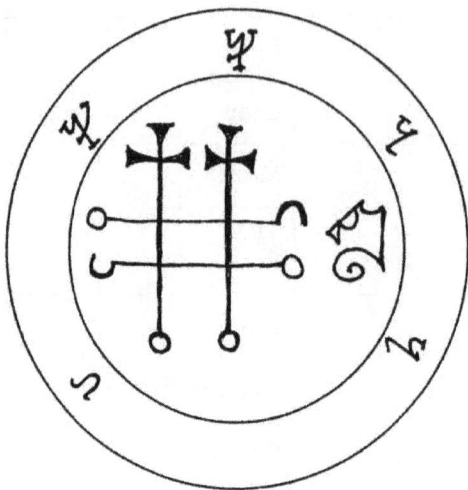

Protects those seeking the true light. Dominates peace treaties and influences ambassadors.

Angelic conjuration:

>'Clamavi in toto corde meo exaudi me Domine Justificationes meas requiram.'

>'I have called unto thee with all my heart Hear me O Lord and I shall seek my justification.'

Psalm 119:145

Ronove

Rank	Marquis
Ruler	Goap
Archangel	Mikael
Sign	♌ 10°-14°
Direction	East
Sigil colour	Blue and green
Incense	Cedar and rose
Metal	Silver
Time of conjuration	3pm till sunrise

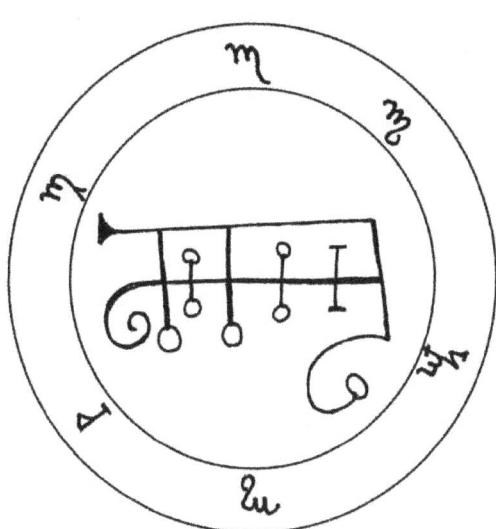

Ronove is the twenty-seventh spirit and appears as a monster. He will teach rhetoric very well and gives good servants. He grants knowledge of tongues and favours with friends or foes. He is as a marquis and a great earl who has under his command 19 spirits.

Binding Angel: Yerathel

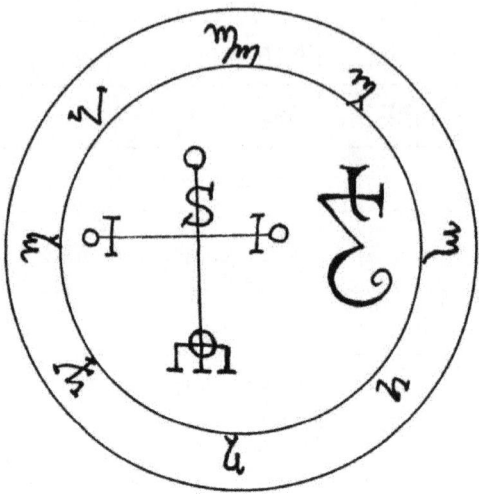

Protects against unjust attacks. Confounds one's enemies and dominates civilisations, also dominates peace.

Angelic conjuration:

'Eripe me Domine ab homine malo a viro iniquo eripe me.'

'Save me O Lord from the evil man and deliver me from the wicked doer.'

Psalm 140:2

Berith

Rank	Duke
Ruler	Goap
Archangel	Mikael
Sign	♌ 15°-19°
Direction	East
Incense	Cedar and rose
Sigil colour	Blue and green
Metal	Copper
Time of conjuration	Sunrise to noon in clear weather

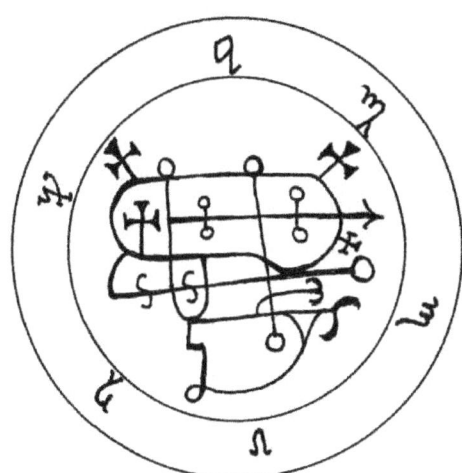

Berith is the twenty-eighth spirit and he is a mighty duke. He also answers to two other names, Beal and Bolfrey. He will appear as a soldier wearing red and riding upon a red horse. He wears a gold crown and will give true answers past, present and to come. The conjuror must use the ring when conjuring this spirit. He can turn all metal into gold, he also grants dignities and confirms them too. He will speak with a clear and subtle voice and is a great liar and not to be trusted. He governs 26 legions of spirits.

Binding Angel: Sheahiah

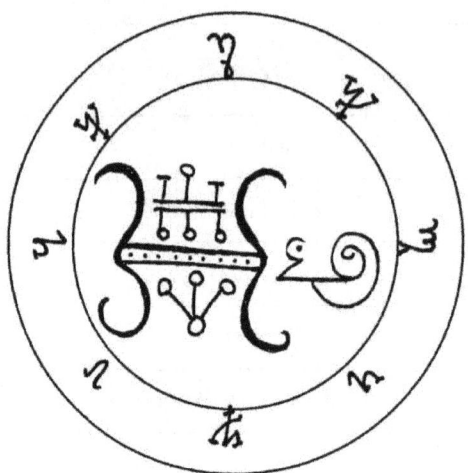

Protects against fire, ruin and collapse. Dominates health and long life, will also promote prudence.

Angelic conjuration:

> '*Deus ne elongeris a me*
> *Deus meus in auxilium meum respice.*'

> 'Let not God depart from me Look to my help O God.'

Psalm 71:12

Astaroth

Rank	Duke
Ruler	Goap
Archangel	Mikael
Sign	♌ 20°-24°
Direction	East
Incense	Dragon's blood and cedar
Sigil colour	Blue and red
Metal	Copper
Time of conjuration	Sunrise until noon in clear weather

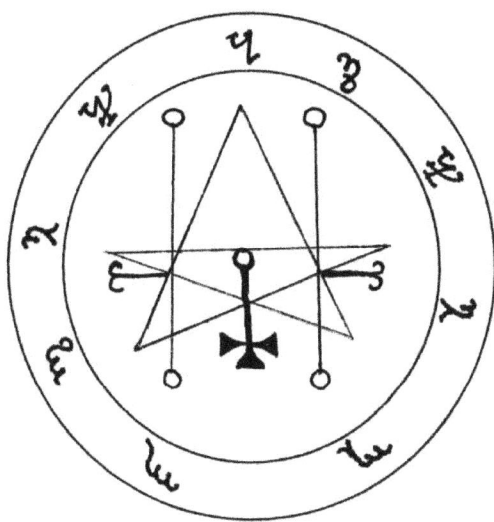

The twenty-ninth spirit is Astaroth who is a mighty and strong duke, who appears as an angel riding upon a dragon and carries a viper in his right hand. The conjuror must hold the ring near his face to avert the breath of the spirit as it will be harmful. He will give true answers of things past, present and to come. He can show all secrets and will tell how the spirits fell and the reason of his own fall. He can instruct in all liberal artes and rules 40 legions of spirits.

Binding Angel: Reiyel

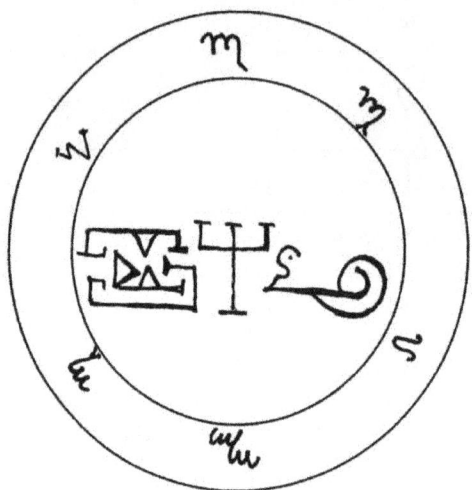

Reiyel will help to protect the conjuror against their enemies, both visible and invisible. The angel dominates mystical experiences and influences peace.

Angelic conjuration:

'Ecce Deus adjuvat me et Dominius susceptor est animae meae.'

'Behold God is my help and the Lord is the guardian of my soul.'
Psalm 54:4

Fornius

Rank	Marquis
Ruler	Goap
Archangel	Mikael
Sign	♌ 25°-29°
Direction	East
Incense	Dragon's blood and jasmine
Sigil colour	Red and silver
Metal	Silver
Time of conjuration	3pm until sunrise

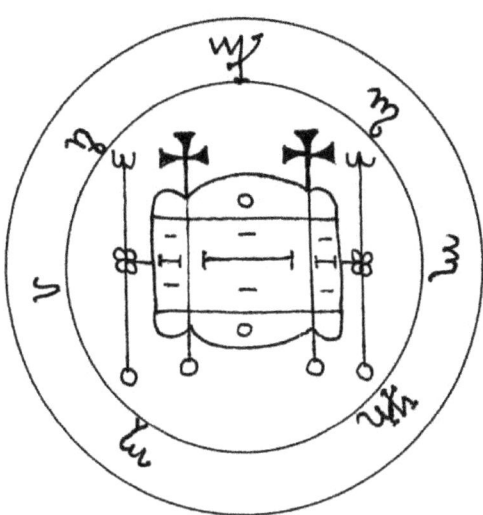

The thirtieth spirit is Fornius also known as Forneus. He is a great marquis who will appear as a sea monster, who will teach rhetoric. He causes men to have a great name and have a knowledge and understanding of all tongues. He will make the conjuror beloved by friend and foe. He governs 29 legions of spirits and is partly of the order of thrones and partly of angels.

Binding Angel: Omael

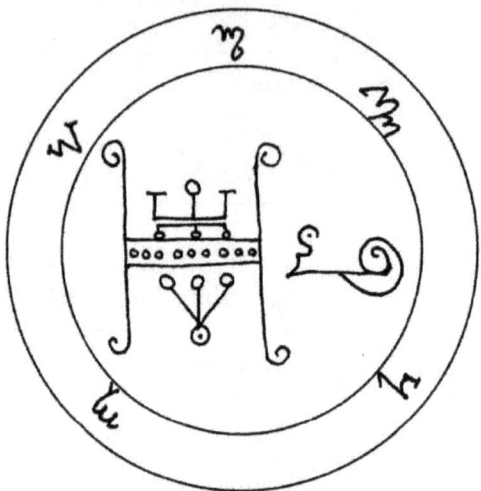

This angel will help against all desperation and troubles, they will also strengthen patience. He also dominates the birth of animals and all men.

Angelic conjuration:

> 'Quoniam tu es potentia mea Domine. Domine spes mea a juventute mea.'

> 'For thou art my strength O Lord,
> O Lord thou art my hope from my youth.'

Psalm 70:6

Foras

Rank	President
Ruler	Ziminiar
Archangel	Auriel
Sign	♍ 0°-4°
Direction	South
Incense	Lavender
Sigil colour	Orange
Metal	Mercury
Time	Anytime except twilight unless the king is invocated first.

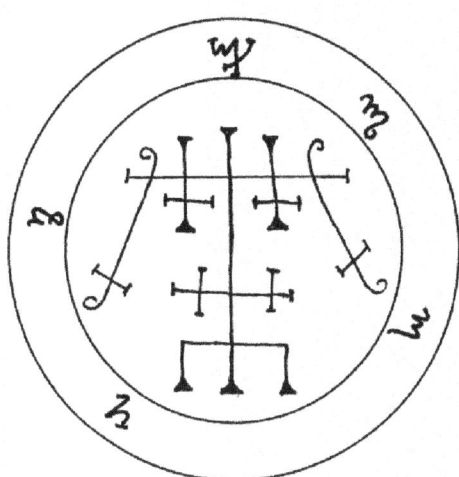

The thirty-first spirit Foras is a mighty president who will appear as a strong man, who will teach the virtue of all herbs and stones. He will also teach ethics and logic. He can also make the conjuror invisible and will also prolong long life and eloquence. He will also discover treasure and lost items.

Binding Angel: Lectabel

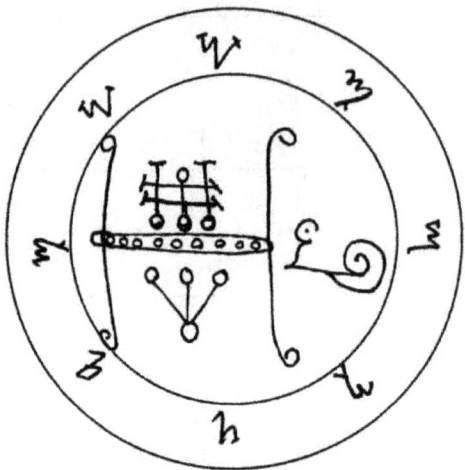

This angel will help the conjuror's profession. They also dominate growth and will help with the study of astrology.

Angelic conjuration:

> 'Introibo in potentiam Domini,
> Deus meus memorabor justitiae tuae solius.'

> 'I shall enter into the power of the Lord my God I shall be mindful of thy justice only.'

Psalm 70:16

Asmoday

Rank	King
Ruler	Ziminiar
Archangel	Auriel
Sign	♍ 5°-9°
Direction	South
Incense	Olibanum and storax
Sigil colour	Gold and orange
Metal	Gold
Time of conjuration	9am until noon and also 3pm until sunset

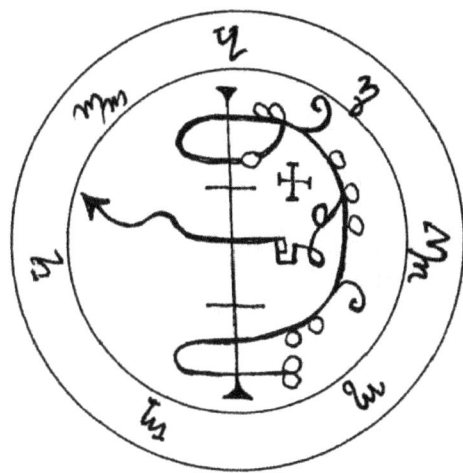

The thirty-second spirit is Asmoday or Asmodai who is a great king, who is strong and powerful. He will appear with three heads whereof the first is like unto a bull, the second like a man and the third like a ram.

He will also have a tail like a serpent and from his mouth comes forth fire. He has webbed feet and sits upon a dragon, he bears in his hand a lance with a banner. He must be addressed by the conjuror with their head uncovered during the operation.

He gives a ring of virtue and geometry, and also will teach arithmetic, astronomy and handicrafts. He will give true and full answers to any question asked and can make the conjuror invincible. He will reveal where treasure lies and who guards it. He governs 72 legions of spirits and is among the legions of Amaymon.

Binding Angel: Vashariah

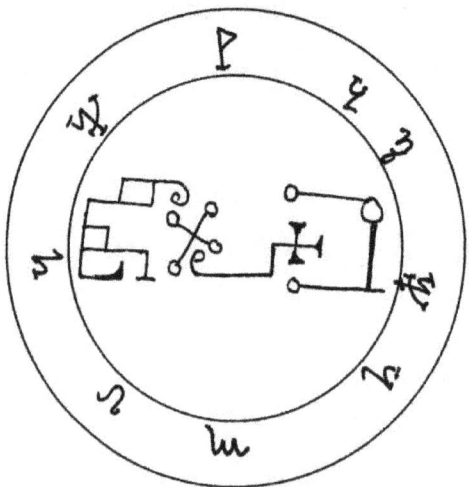

This angel will defend the conjuror against all false accusations and will influence judgement in all cases.

Angelic conjuration:

'Quia rectum est verbum Domini et omnia eius in fide'

'For the word of the Lord is upright, and all his works faithful'

Psalm 33.4

Gaap

Rank	President
Ruler	Ziminiar
Archangel	Auriel
Sign	♍ 10°-14°
Direction	South
Incense	Myrrh and storax
Sigil colour	Black and orange
Metal	Mercury
Time of conjuration	Anytime except twilight unless the king is invoked first.

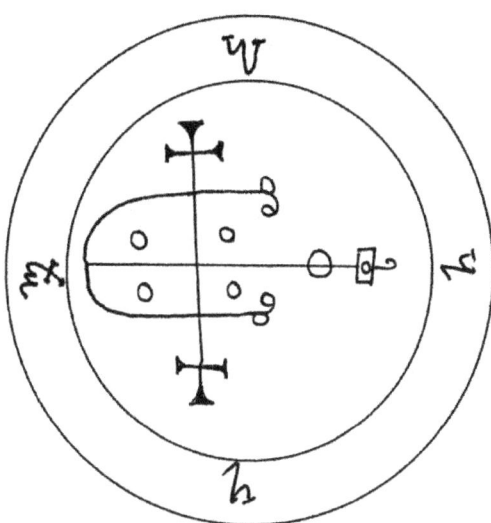

The thirty-third spirit is a mighty president and prince. He will appear when the sun enters the southern signs. He will appear as a man standing before four kings and his office is to make men insensible and ignorant. But he will also make them knowing in all liberal arts and philosophy and will cause both love and hate. He will also deliver the familiars of other magicians unto the conjuror and will also answer all questions of the past, present and the future truthfully. He will also transport the conjuror from one place unto another. He rules 66 legions of spirits and he was of the order of potentates.

Binding Angel: Yechuiah

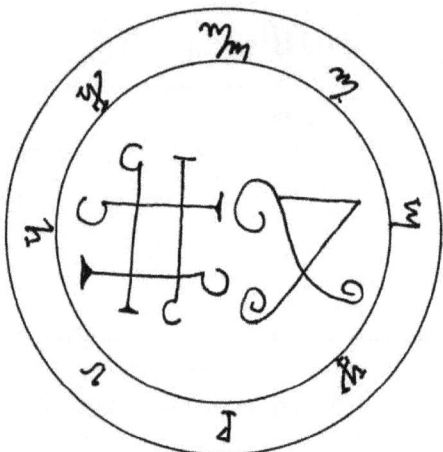

This angel will uncover the plots of those who conspire against the conjuror and will undo their plans. He also influences rulers and those who sit in judgement.

Angelic conjuration:

'Dominus scit cogitations hominum quoniam vana sunt.'

'The Lord knows the thoughts of men for they are in vain.'

Psalm 91:11

Furfur

Rank	Earl
Ruler	King ziminiar
Archangel	Auriel
Sign	♍ 15°-19°
Direction	South
Incense	Myrrh and pepper
Sigil colour	Black and red
Metal	Copper or silver
Time of Conjuration	Any hour of the day

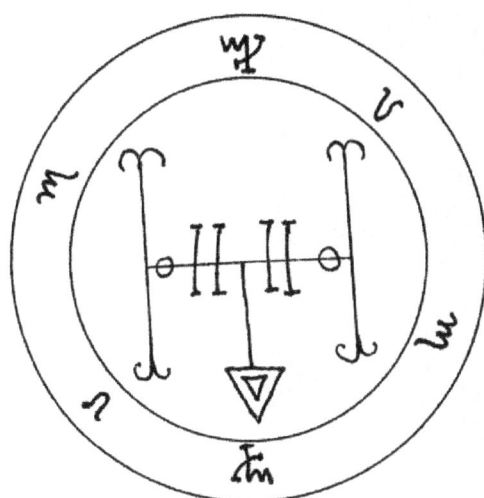

The thirty-fourth spirit is Furfur and he is a great and mighty earl, who appears in the form of a hart with a fiery tail. He will not speak truly unless the conjuror constrains the spirit within the triangle of arte. He will then appear as an angel who speaks with a hoarse voice. He causes love between man and woman. He will cause lightning and thunder, blasts and great storms. Also he will answer all manner of questions that the conjuror may ask. He rules over 26 legions of spirits.

Binding Angel: Lehachiah

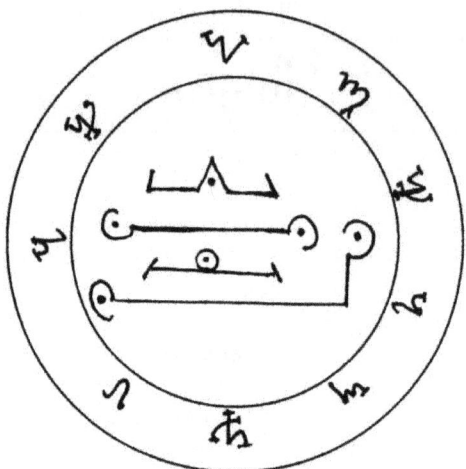

The angel will help to maintain peace and harmony. He will also promote faithfulness and respect from people.

Angelic conjuration:

> *'Speret Israel in Domino*
> *ex hoc nunc et usque in saeculum.'*

'Let Israel hope in the Lord from this time forth and for evermore.'

Psalm 131:3

Marchosias

Rank	Marquis
Ruler	Ziminiar
Archangel	Auriel
Sign	♍ 20°-24°
Direction	South
Incense	Red and white sandal
Sigil colour	Green and purple
Metal	Silver
Time of conjuration	3pm until sunrise

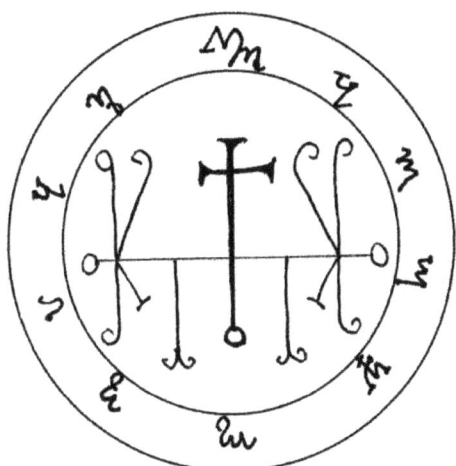

The thirty-fifth spirit is Marchosias and he is mighty marquis, who appears at first like a great wolf having gryphon's wings and a serpent's tail. He vomits forth fire. But at the command of the conjuror he will assume human form, who is a strong fighter. He was of the order of

Dominations and he governs 30 legions of spirits.

Binding Angel: Kavakiah

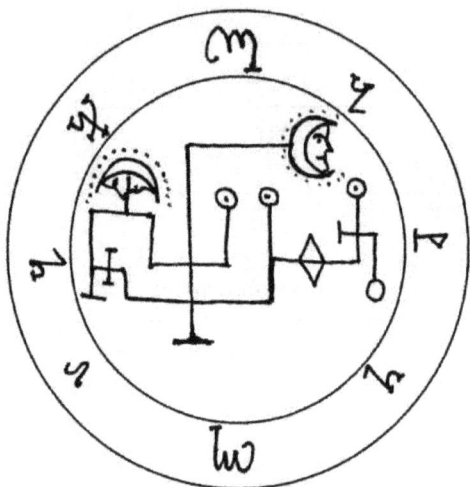

Recovers the friendship of those who we have offended and dominates wills.

Angelic conjuration:

'Dilexi quoniam exaudi Dominus vocem orationis meae.'

'I am joyful for the Lord hears the voice of my prayer.'

Psalm 116:1

Stolas

Rank	Prince
Ruler	Ziminiar
Archangel	Auriel
Sign	♍ 25°-29°
Direction	South
Incense	Rose and red sandal
Sigil colour	Green
Metal	Tin
Time of conjuration	Any hour of the day

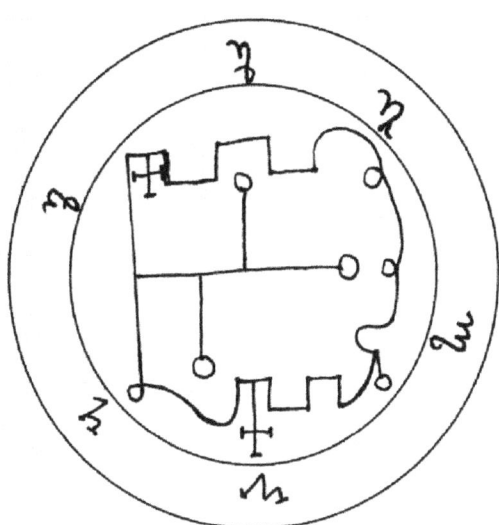

Stolas is the thirty-sixth spirit and is a great and powerful prince, who will at first appear as a mighty raven but at the command of the conjuror will take on the form of a man. His office is to teach, and also the virtue of herb and stones. He governs 26 legions of spirits.

Binding Angel: Monadel

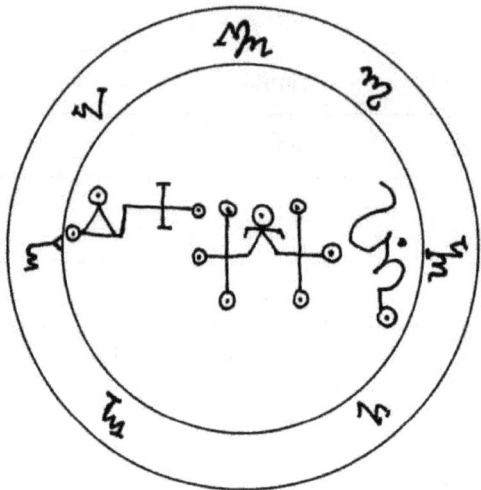

This angel will protect against slander and will also release prisoners. He will also help exiles to return to their homes.

Angelic conjuration:

> 'Domine dilexi decorum Domus tuae et locum habitationis gloriae tuae.'

> 'I have delighted in the beauty of thy house O Lord and in the place of the habitation of thy glory.'

Psalm 26:8

Phenex

Rank	Marquis
Ruler	Amaymon
Archangel	Raphael
Sign	♎ 0°-4°
Direction	West
Incense	Rose and sandal
Sigil colour	Green and purple
Metal	Silver
Time of conjuration	3pm until sunrise

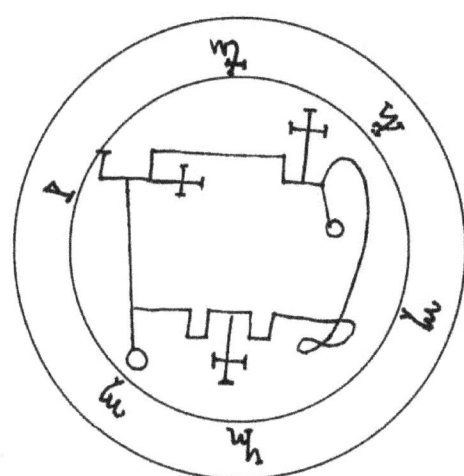

This spirit is the thirty-seventh spirit of the Goetia and is a great marquis who will appear as a phoenix bird having the voice of a child. At the command of the conjuror the spirit will assume human form; their office is to teach all of the sciences. He is also a good poet and will willingly perform all the requests of the conjuror. He has 20 legions of spirits under his command.

Binding Angel: Aniel

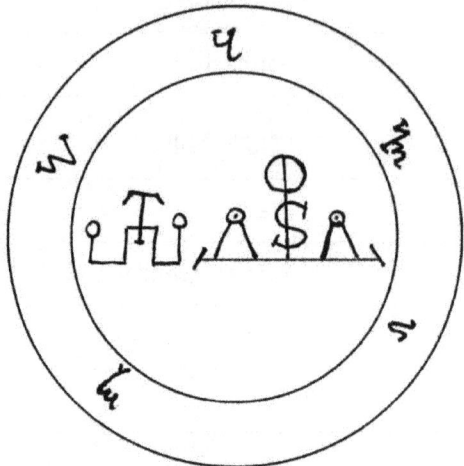

The thirty-seventh angel of the Schemhamephorasch will help to conquer and to gain release from siege. This angel will also dominate the arts and sciences; he also influences the meditations of the wise.

Angelic conjuration:

> 'Domini Deus virtutum converte nos et ostende faciem tuam et salvi erimus.'

> 'O Lord God turn thy power towards us and show us thy face and we shall be saved.'

Psalm 90:20

Halphas

Rank	Earl
Ruler	Amaymon
Archangel	Raphael
Sign	♎ 5°-9°
Direction	West
Incense	Red sandal and dragon's blood
Sigil colour	Green and red
Metal	Copper or silver
Time of conjuration	Any hour of the day

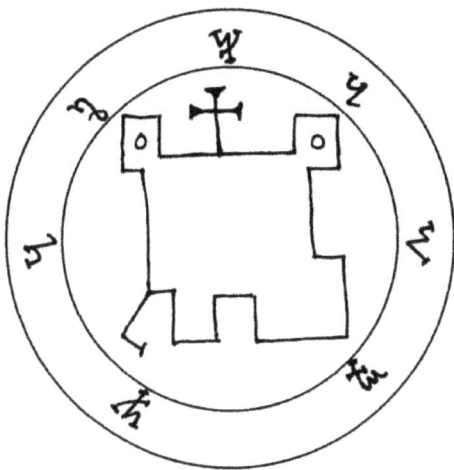

The thirty-eighth spirit is Halpas and he is a great earl who will appear as a dove. He will speak with a hoarse voice, and his office is to build up towers and to provide arms and men of war. He rules over 26 legions of spirits.

Binding Angel: Chaamiah

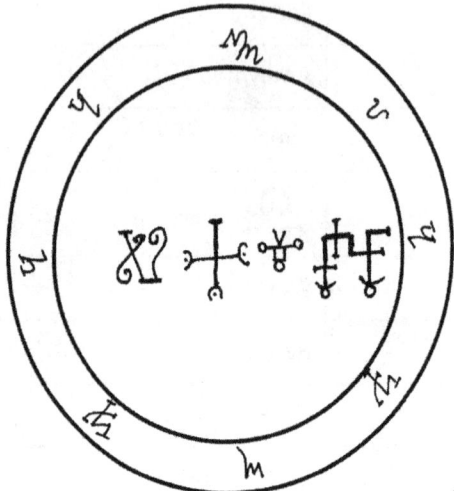

This angel will protect the conjuror from the infernal spirits and also lightning too. The angel will help and protect those who seek the truth.

Angelic conjuration:

> 'Quoniam tu es Domine spes mea altissimum profuisti refugium tuum.'

> 'For thou art my hope, O Lord and thou hast been my deepest refuge.'

Psalm 90:9

Malphas

Rank	President
Ruler	Amaymon
Archangel	Raphael
Sign	♎ 10°-14°
Direction	West
Incense	Lavender and myrrh
Sigil colour	Orange and black
Metal	Mercury
Time of conjuration	Any time except twilight at night, unless the king is invoked first

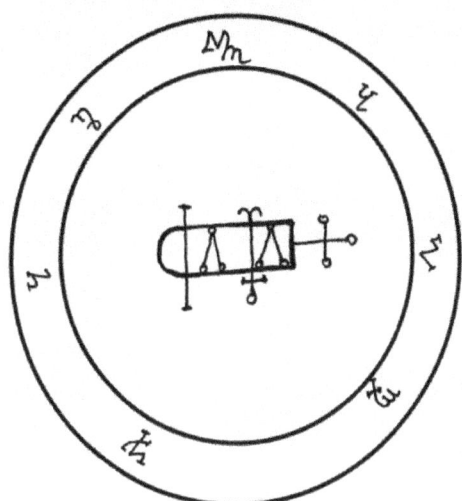

Malphas, who is the thirty-ninth spirit, traditionally appears as a crow but at the command of the conjuror he will adopt human form; he can also speak with a hoarse voice too. His office is to build houses and high towers, but he can also reveal the plans of your enemies and opponents. He gives good familiars and will be pleased with any sacrifice that you make, however if you do so tradition considers that he will deceive the conjuror.

Binding Angel: Rehael

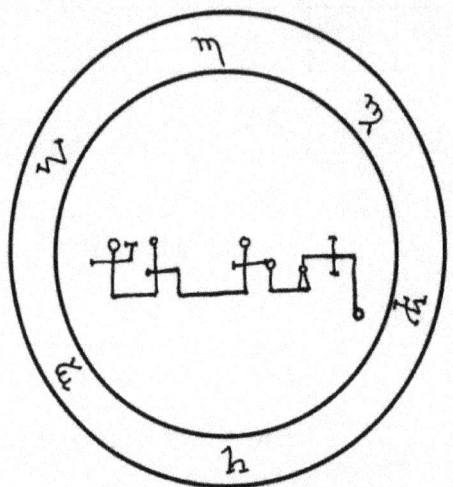

The thirty-ninth binding angel protects against disease and will also cure the same. He promotes health and longevity, and will also influence paternal love.

Angelic conjuration:

> 'Audivit Dominus et misertus est mihi Dominus factus est adiutor meus.'

'The Lord has heard me and pitied me and the Lord is my helper.'

Psalm 30:11

Raum

Rank	Earl
Ruler	Amaymon
Archangel	Raphael
Sign	♎ 15°-19°
Direction	West
Incense	Myrrh and dragon's blood
Sigil colour	Black and red
Metal	Copper or silver
Time of conjuration	Any hour of the day

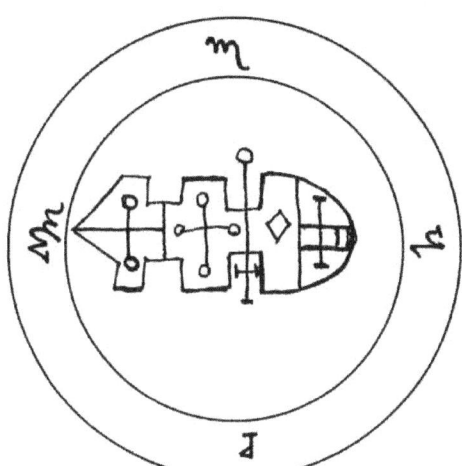

The fortieth spirit is Raum and he is a great earl who will appear at first in the form of a crow. However at the command of the conjuror he will assume human form. He will steal treasure out of the King's house and will carry it where he is commanded. He will destroy cities and the dignity of men. He will tell of all things past, present and to come. He will also cause love between friend and foe. Before his fall he was of the order of thrones and he governs 30 legions.

Binding Angel: Yeiazel

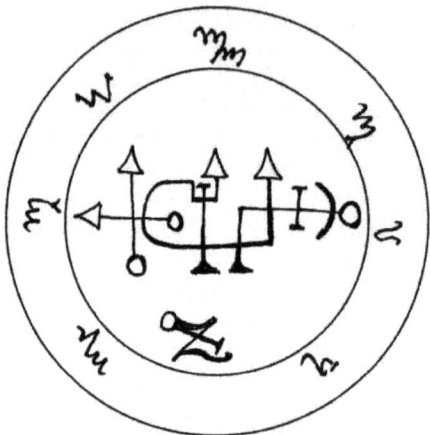

This angel will help to secure the release of prisoners and also the release from enemies. He will also influence the world of books and the press; he is also useful in helping artists with their work.

Angelic conjuration:

> 'Ut quid Domine repellis animam meam avertis faciem tuam a me.'

> 'Why drivest thou away my soul O Lord and turnest thy face from me?'

Psalm 98:15

Focalor

Rank	Duke
Ruler	Amaymon
Archangel	Raphael
Sign	♎ 20°-24°
Direction	West
Incense	Lavender and rose
Sigil colour	Green and orange
Metal	Copper
Time of conjuration	Sunrise until noon in clear weather

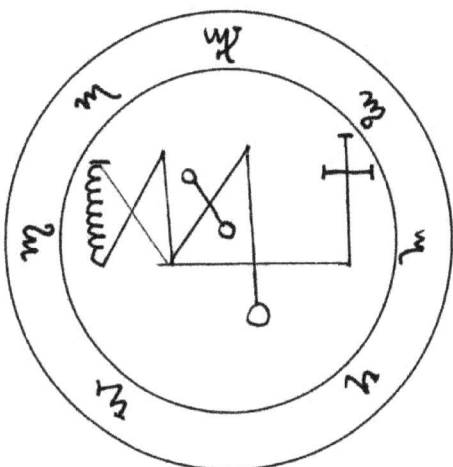

Focalor is the forty-first spirit and he is a strong and mighty duke, who will appear in the form of a man with gryphon's wings. His office is to slay men and also to drown them. He will overthrow ships of war as he has power over wind and the sea. But he will not hurt any if the conjuror commands him so. He governs 30 legions of spirits

Binding Angel: Hahahel

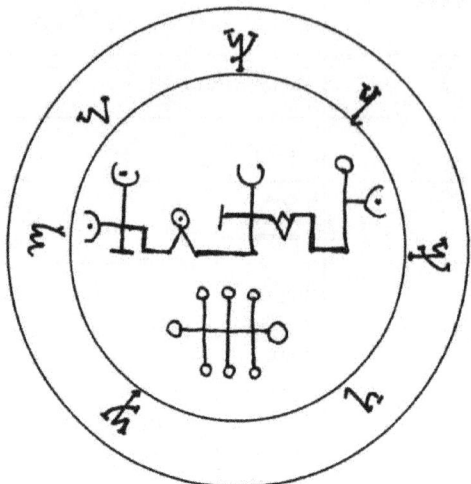

This angel will help against the ungodly and will counteract slanders. Will also be helpful to priests and prelates.

Angelic conjuration:

'Domine libera animam meam a labiis iniquis et a lingua dolosa.'

'O Lord deliver my soul from wicked lips and a deceitful tongue.'

Psalm 12:4

Vepar

Rank	Duke
Ruler	Amaymon
Archangel	Raphael
Sign	♎ 25°-29°
Direction	West
Incense	Storax and red sandal
Sigil colour	Orange and green
Metal	Copper
Time of conjuration	Sunrise until noon in clear weather

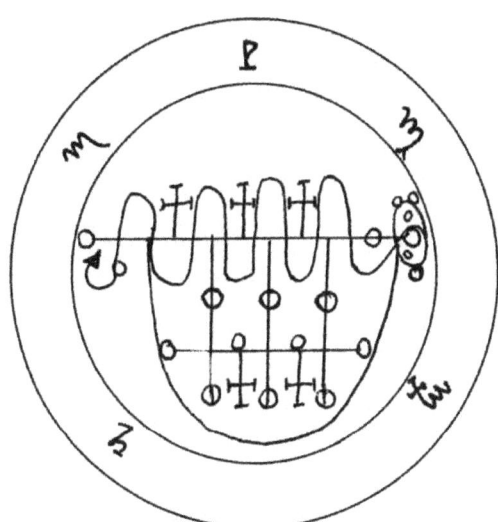

Vepar is the forty-second spirit and he is a great duke who will appear as a mermaid. His office is to govern the waters and to guide ships laden with arms. He can cause the sea to appear full of ships all with men on board. He will cause men to die in three days from putrefying wounds, or sores. He governs 29 legions of spirits.

Binding Angel: Mikael

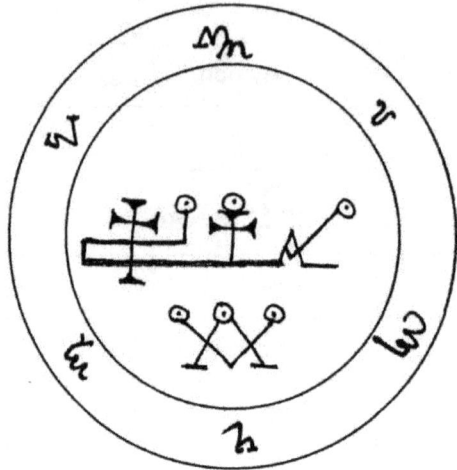

This angel will help protect travellers on their journeys, and is influential upon the powerful and politics.

Angelic conjuration:

'Domine custodit te ab omni malo Et custodiet animam tuam.'

'The Lord protects thee from all evil and will protect thy soul.'

Psalm 121:7

Sabnock

Rank	Marquis
Ruler	Corson
Archangel	Gabriel
Sign	♏ 0°-4°
Direction	North
Incense	Dragon's blood and jasmine
Sigil colour	Red and purple
Metal	Silver
Time of conjuration	3pm until sunrise

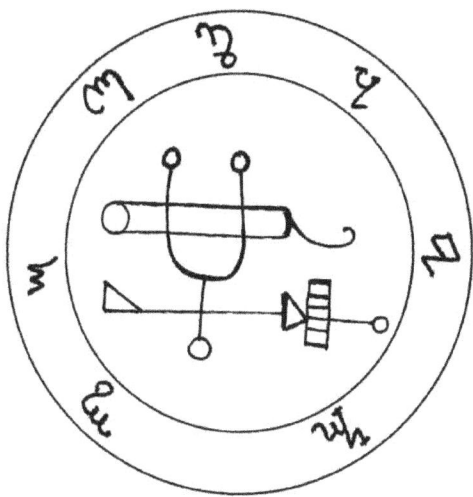

Sabnock is the forty-third spirit that was commanded by King Solomon into the vessel of brass and he is a great and mighty marquis. He appears as an armed soldier with a lion's head and he rides upon a pale horse. His office is to build castles, cities and towers. He will furnish them with arms and armour; he will also at the conjuror's command inflict wounds and sores upon those whom the conjuror should so will. He grants good and reliable familiars, and rules over 50 legions of spirits.

Binding Angel: Vevaliah

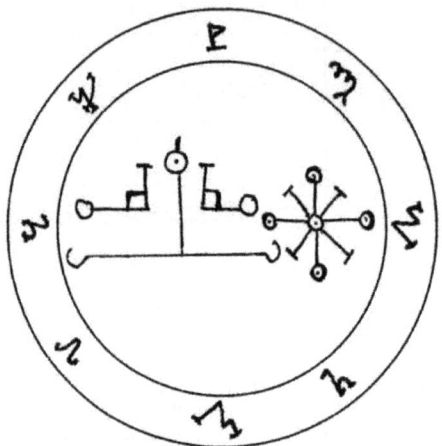

This angel will help to destroy enemies and will also free slaves. Also dominates peace and influences prosperity.

Angelic conjuration:

> 'Et ego ad te Domine clamavit
> Et mane oratio meae praeveniet te.'

> 'I have cried unto thee O Lord and let my prayer come unto thee.'

Psalm 88:14

Shax

Rank	Marquis
Ruler	Corson
Archangel	Gabriel
Sign	♏ 5°-9°
Direction	North
Incense	Pepper and lotus
Sigil colour	Red and purple
Metal	Silver
Time of conjuration	3pm until sunrise

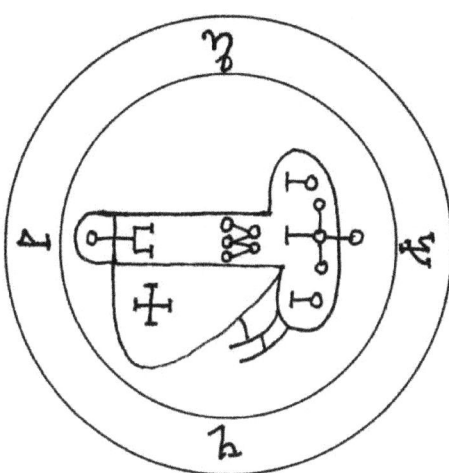

The forty-fourth spirit is Shax and he is a great marquis who appears as a stock dove speaking with a subtle voice. His office is to take away the sight, hearing or understanding of any man or woman that the conjuror demands. He will also steal money out of the houses of the king and carry it where the conjuror should will. If commanded he will also fetch horses or any other thing that the conjuror demands. But he must be conjured into the triangle of arte first, or otherwise he will tell lies. He can also discover all things which are hidden and not kept by wicked spirits. He will give good familiars and he governs 30 legions of spirits.

Binding Angel: Yelahiah

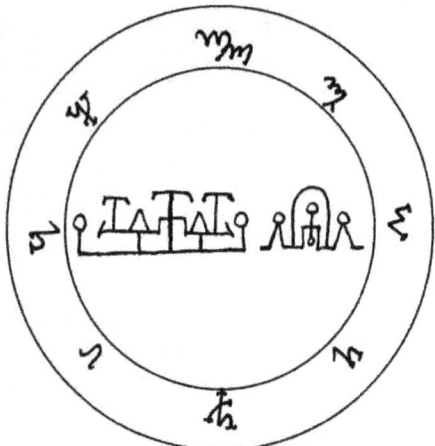

This angel will help win all lawsuits. He also dominates and promotes victory and grants courage in battle.

Angelic conjuration:

'Voluntaria eris mei beneplacita fac Domine et judicia tua doce.'

'Make my wishes pleasing unto thee O Lord and teach me thy judgements.'

Psalm 119:108

Vine

Rank	King
Ruler	Corson
Archangel	Gabriel
Sign	♏ 10°-14°
Direction	North
Incense	Cedar and frankincense
Sigil colour	Blue and gold
Metal	Gold
Time of conjuration	9am – noon 3pm – sunset

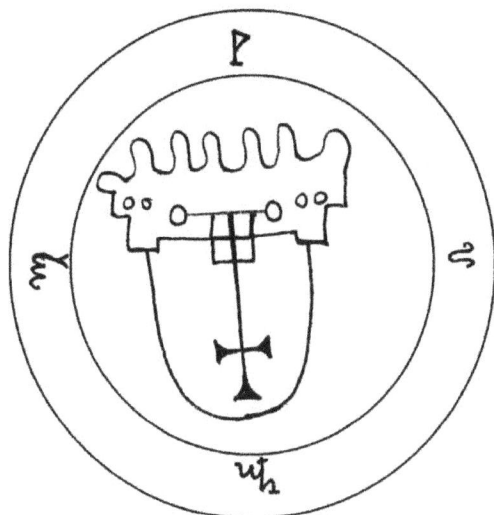

The forty-fifth spirit is Vine who is a great king and earl. He will appear in the form of a lion who rides upon a black horse, he will also bear a viper in his hand. His office is to discover things that are hidden, also witches, wizards and all things that are present, past and to come.

He will at the command of the conjuror build or overthrow towers, stone walls and make the waters rough with storms, he also governs 36 legions of spirits.

Binding Angel: Sealiah

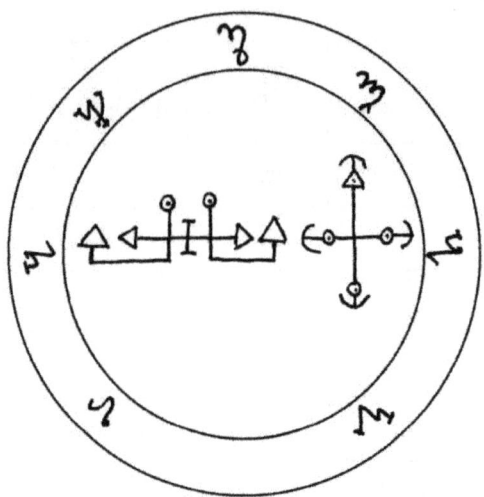

The office of this angel is to confound and confuse the evil and proud. They will also promote education and the growth of vegetation.

Angelic conjuration:

> 'Si dicebam motus est pes meus misericordia tua Domine adiuvabit me.'

> 'If I say that my foot is moved thou wilt help me of thy mercy.'

Psalm 94:18

Bifrons

Rank	Earl
Ruler	Corson
Archangel	Gabriel
Sign	♏ 15°-19°
Direction	North
Incense	Cedar and dragon's blood
Sigil colour	Blue and red
Metal	Copper or silver
Time of conjuration	Any hour of the day

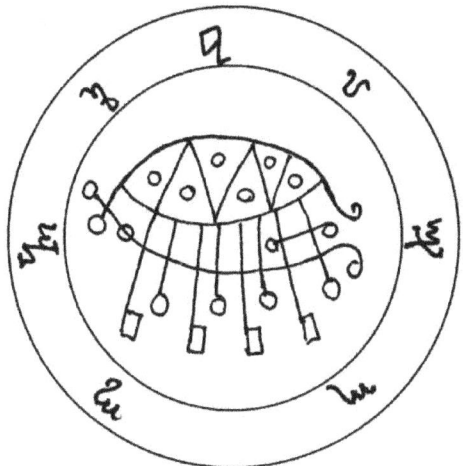

The forty-sixth spirit is called Bifrons and is an earl who appears in the form of a monster. He will assume human form when he is commanded to by the conjuror. His office is to teach astrology, geometry and other artes and sciences. He will also teach the virtue of herb, precious stones and woods. He will change the places of the dead and will also light candles over the graves of the dead. He commands 60 legions of spirits.

Binding Angel: Ariel

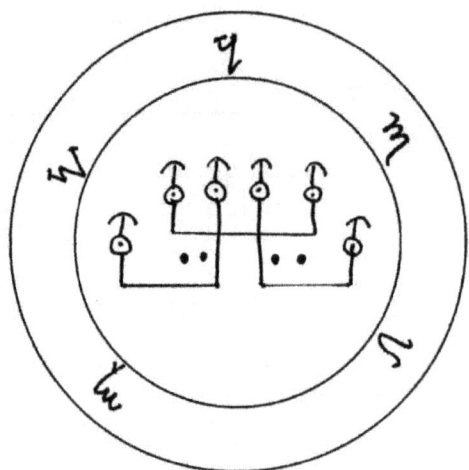

This angel will help to reveal hidden treasure and will also dominate night time visions. He will also influence favourably difficult situations.

Angelic conjuration:

'*Suavis Dominus universis et miserationes super omnia opera eius.*'

'The Lord is pleasant to all the world and his mercies are over all his works.'

Psalm 145:9

Uvall

Rank	Duke
Ruler	Corson
Archangel	Gabriel
Sign	♏ 20°-24°
Direction	North
Incense	Jasmine and rose
Sigil colour	Green and purple
Metal	Copper
Time of conjuration	Sunrise until noon in clear weather

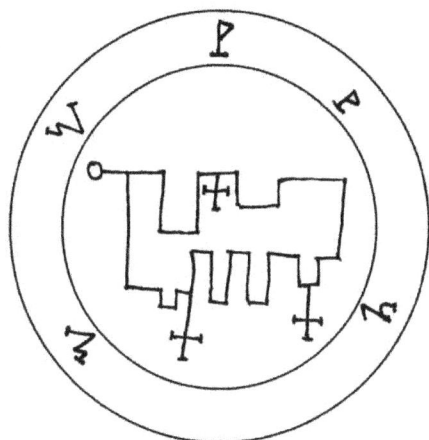

Uvall is the forty-seventh spirit and he is a great duke who appears in the form of a mighty dromedary. At the command of the conjuror he will adopt human form and speaking the Egyptian tongue. His office is to procure the love of women and to foretell the past, present and the future. He will also cause friendship between foes. He was of the order of potentates and he governs 37 legions of spirits.

Binding Angel: Asaliah

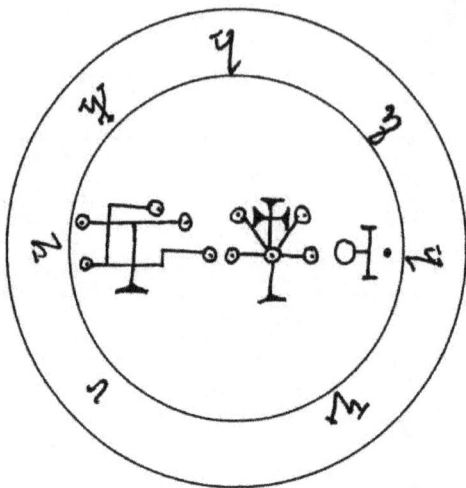

The angel Asaliah will help to assist those who wish to raise themselves spiritually. They also dominate justice and influence contemplations.

Angelic conjuration:

> *'Quam magnificata sunt opera tua Domine nimis profundae factae sunt cogitationes tuae.*
>
> *'How wonderful are thy works*
> *O Lord and how deep are thy thoughts.'*

Psalm 92:6

Haagenti

Rank	President
Ruler	Corson
Archangel	Gabriel
Sign	♏ 25°-29°
Direction	North
Incense	Lavender and jasmine
Sigil colour	Orange and purple
Metal	Mercury
Time of conjuration	Anytime apart from twilight unless their King is invoked first

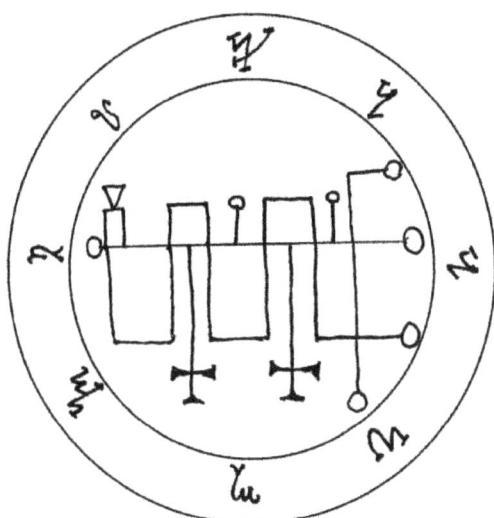

The forty-eighth spirit is Haagenti who is a mighty president who appears in the form of a bull with gryphon's wings. He will assume human form at the command of the conjuror. His office is to make men wise and to instruct them in divers matters. He will also transmute all metals into gold and will also change water into wine and vice-versa. He governs 33 legions of spirits.

Binding Angel: Mihael

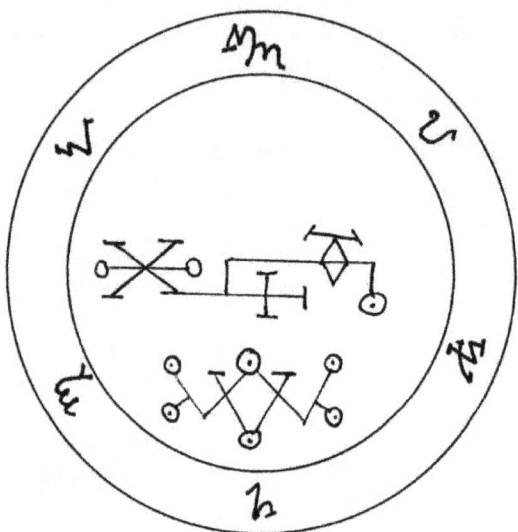

This angel will help to preserve harmony and union between spouses; he dominates the generations and influences love.

Angelic conjuration:

'Notum fecit Dominus salutare tuum
in conspectu gentium revelabit justitiam suam'

'The Lord hath made thy salvation known in the sight of the peoples and will reveal his justice.'

Psalm 98:2

Crocell

Rank	Duke
Ruler	Goap
Archangel	Mikael
Sign	♐ 0°-4°
Direction	East
Incense	Cedar and rose
Sigil colour	Blue and green
Metal	Copper
Time of conjuration	Sunrise to noon in clear weather

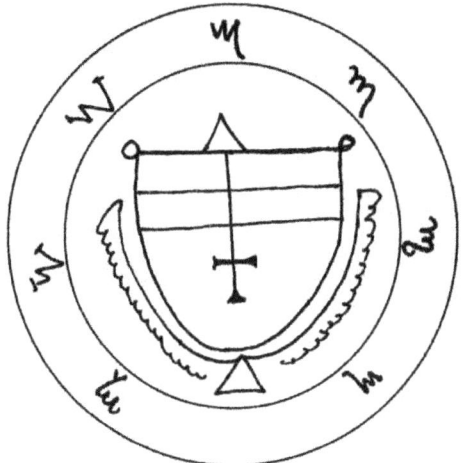

Crocell is the forty-ninth spirit and will appear as an angel. He is a great duke who will speak mystically of hidden things and will teach geometry and liberal sciences. He will at the command of the conjuror, make rushing noises of water and will warm bath waters, and will also discover baths too. He was of the order of powers before his fall and he governs 48 legions.

Binding Angel: Vehuel

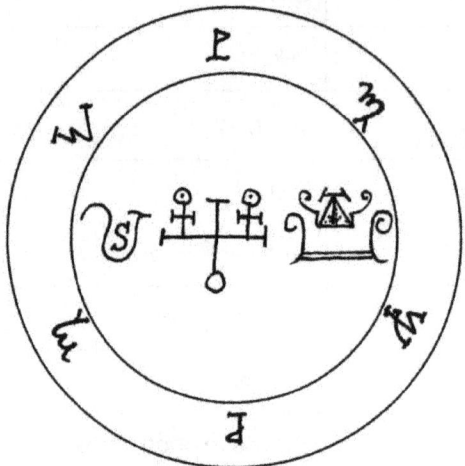

The angel Vehuel will help to grant peace when troubled, and will also influence people and humility.

Angelic conjuration:

'Magnus Domine et laudabilis et magnitudinis eius non est finis.'

'Great is the Lord and worthy to be praised and there is no end to his greatness.'

Psalm 145:3

Furcas

Rank	Knight
Ruler	Goap
Archangel	Mikael
Sign	♐ 5°-9°
Direction	East
Incense	Cedar and myrrh
Sigil colour	Black and blue
Metal	Lead
Time of conjuration	Dawn until sunrise and 4pm until sunset

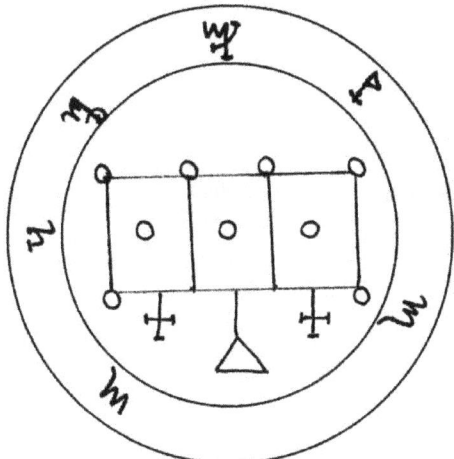

Furcas is the fiftieth spirit and is a knight who appears as a cruel old man, with a long beard and a hoary head. He rides upon a pale horse with a sharp weapon in his hand. His office is to teach the artes of philosophy, astrology, rhetoric, logic, chiromancy and pyromancy in all their parts. He has 20 legions at his command.

Binding Angel: Daniel

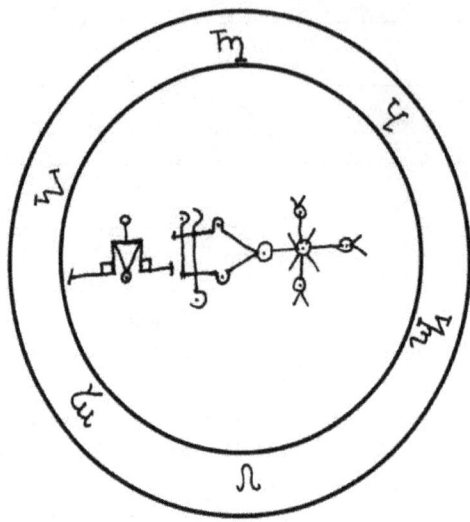

The angel Daniel will console and inspire decisions, he will also influence justice and influences judges.

Angelic conjuration:

'Miserator et misericors Dominus patiens et multum misericors.'

'The Lord is pitiful and merciful long suffering and of great goodness.'

Psalm 15:9

Balam

Rank	King
Ruler	Goap
Archangel	Mikael
Sign	♐ 10°-14°
Direction	East
Incense	Dragon's blood and frankincense
Sigil colour	Red and gold
Metal	Gold
Time of conjuration	9am until noon and 3pm till sunset

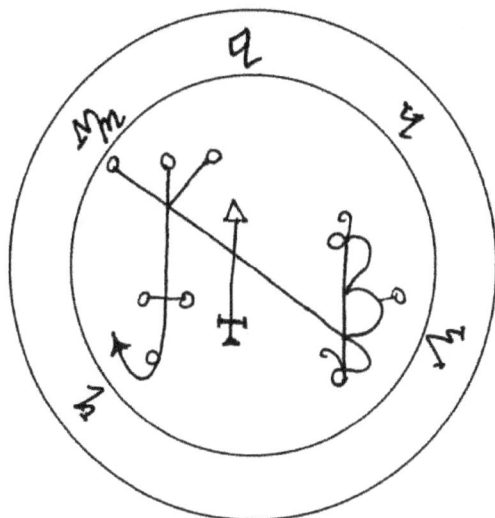

Balam is the fifty-first spirit and he is great and terrible. He is a mighty king who will appear with three heads. The first is like a bull, the second is like that of a man and the third will appear as a ram. He has the tail of a serpent and flaming eyes. He rides upon a furious bear and carries a goshawk upon his fist and speaks with a hoarse voice. His office is to give true answers of things past, present and things to come. He grants invisibility and makes men witty. He governs 40 legions of spirits.

Binding Angel: Hahasiah

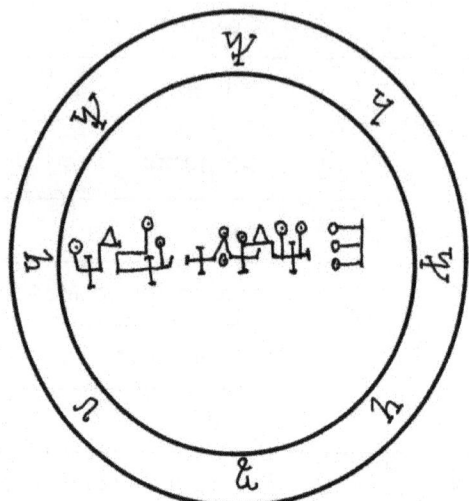

This angel will help those who wish to understand the mysteries of the occult. He also dominates chemistry and abstract sciences.

Angelic conjuration:

> 'Sit gloria Dominus in saeculum laetabitur Dominus in operibus suis.'

> 'Let the Lord be in glory forever and the Lord will rejoice in his works.'

Psalm 104:31

Alloces

Rank	Duke
Ruler	Goap
Archangel	Mikael
Sign	♐ 15°-19°
Direction	East
Incense	Pepper and rose
Sigil colour	Red and green
Metal	Copper
Time of conjuration	From sunrise until noon in clear weather

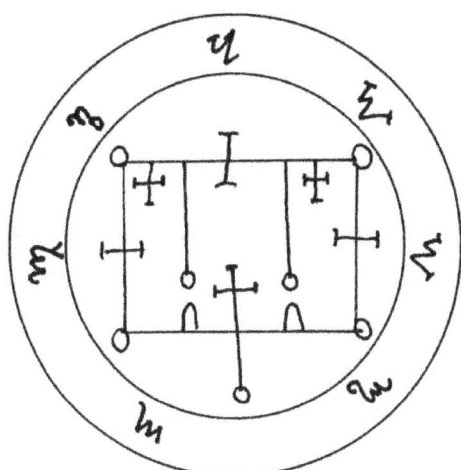

Alloces is the fifty-second spirit and he is a mighty and strong duke who appears as a soldier, who rides upon a great horse. His face is like that of a lion, very red and having eyes of fire. He speaks in a hoarse voice. His office is to teach the artes of astronomy and all liberal sciences. He grants good familiars and rules over 36 legions of spirits.

Binding Angel: Emamiah

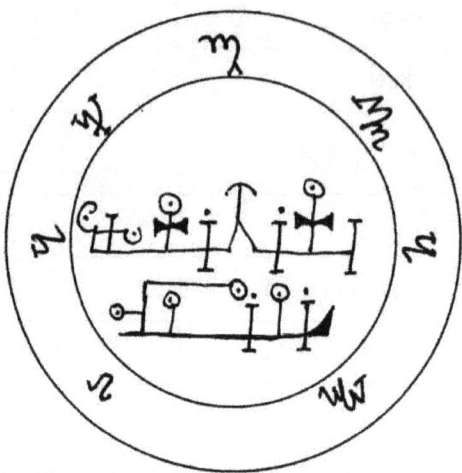

This angel will destroy the enemies of the conjuror, and will also protect prisoners. He also dominates vigour and influences research.

Angelic conjuration:

> 'Confitebor Domino sacundum justitiam eius et psallam nomini Domini altissimi.'

> 'I shall know the Lord according to his justice and shall sing hymns to the name of the Lord, the Greatest.'

Psalm 7:18

Camio

Rank	President
Ruler	Goap
Archangel	Mikael
Sign	♐ 20°-24°
Direction	East
Incense	Frankincense and lavender
Sigil colour	Blue and gold
Metal	Mercury
Time of conjuration	Anytime except twilight unless the king has been invoked first

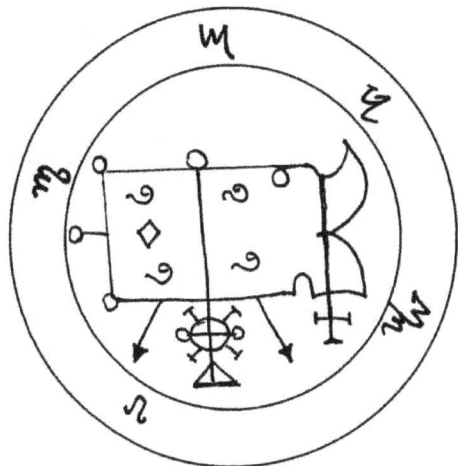

Camio is the fifty-third spirit also known as Caim. He is a great president who appears as a thrush. At the command of the conjuror he will put on the shape of a man who is carrying a sharp sword. He will appear to answer the conjuror through burning coals of fire and is a great disputer. His office is to grant unto men the understanding of all birds, the lowing of cattle and the barking of dogs, and also the language of all animals. He will also give understanding of the voices of water. He will also give true answers to all things that are to come. He was of the order of angels and he rules 30 legions of spirits.

Binding Angel: Nanael

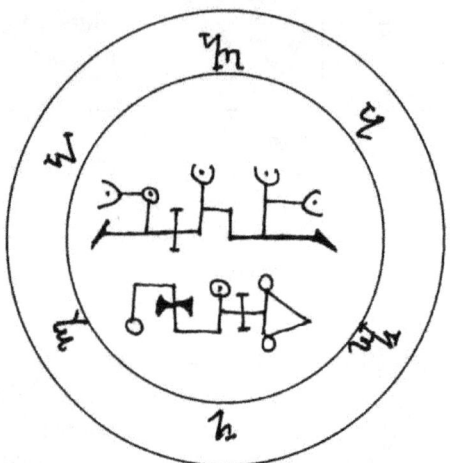

This angel will grant enlightenment and will also dominate the higher sciences. He will also influence teachers and lawyers.

Angelic conjuration:

'Cognovi Domine quia indicia tua iustasunt, et in veritate ego sum humiliabitur'

'I have known thee O Lord for thy judgements are just and in thy truth have I abased myself.'

Psalm 119:75

Murmur

Rank	Duke
Ruler	Goap
Archangel	Mikael
Sign	♐ 25°-29°
Direction	East
Incense	Frankincense and rose
Sigil colour	Green and gold
Metal	Copper
Time of conjuration	Sunrise until noon in clear weather

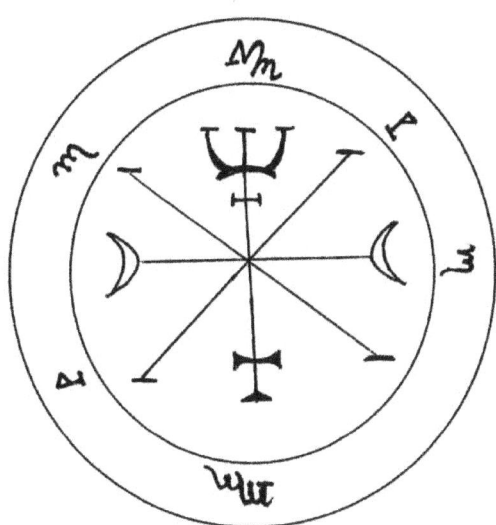

Murmur is the fifty-fourth spirit and is a great duke who appears as a warrior wearing a crown upon his head and riding upon a gryphon. Before go his ministers blowing trumpets. His office is to teach philosophy and to constrain the dead to come before the conjuror to answer questions. He was partly of the order of thrones and partly of angels. He rules 30 legions of spirits.

Binding Angel: Nithael

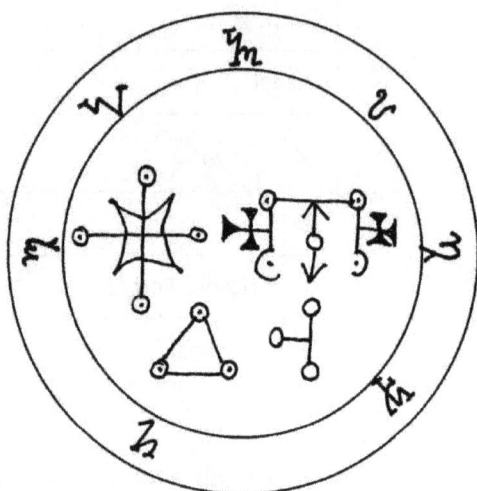

This angel will promote longevity and mercy; he will also dominate dynasties and stability.

Angelic conjuration:

> 'Dominus in caelo paravit sedem suam et regnum suum omnibus dominabitur.'

> 'The Lord hath prepared his seat in heaven and his rule shall be over all.'

Psalm 103:19

Orobas

Rank	Prince
Ruler	Ziminiar
Archangel	Auriel
Sign	♑ 0°-4°
Direction	South
Incense	Myrrh and cedar
Sigil colour	Black and blue
Metal	Tin
Time of conjuration	Any hour of the day

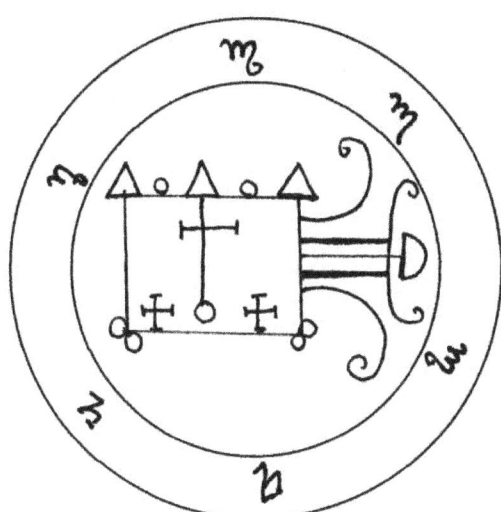

Orobas is the fifty-fifth spirit and is a great and mighty Prince. He will appear at first like a horse who will at the command of the conjuror change into human shape. His office is to discover all things past, present and to come. He can also grant dignities and prelacies, and the favours of friend and foe alike. He will give true answers regarding all matters of divinity and the creation of the world. He is faithful unto the conjuror and will not suffer him to be tempted by any spirit. He governs 20 legions of spirits.

Binding Angel: Mebahiah

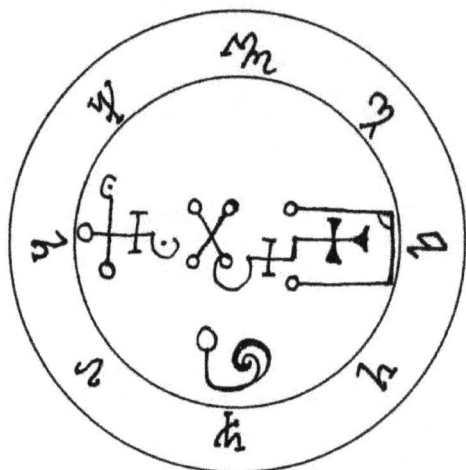

This angel will promote fertility and child birth. He will also help console those who suffer and also dominates morality, religion and piety.

Angelic conjuration:

> 'Tu autem Domine in aeternum Domini memoriale in generationem et generationem'

> 'Thou remainest forever O Lord and thy memorial is from generation unto generation.'

Psalm 102:13

Gremory

Rank	Duke
Ruler	Ziminiar
Archangel	Auriel
Sign	♑ 5°-9°
Direction	South
Incense	Myrrh and red sandal
Sigil colour	Black and green
Metal	Copper
Time of conjuration	From sunrise until noon in clear weather

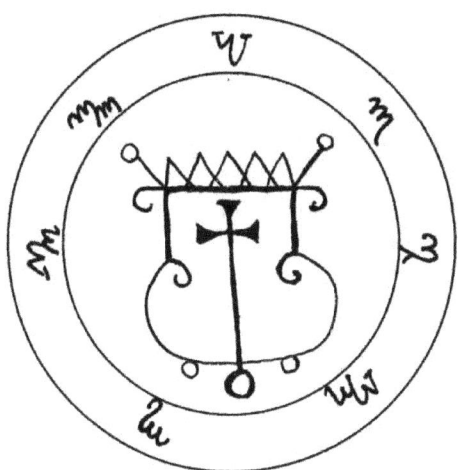

The fifty-sixth spirit is Gremory and he is a powerful and strong duke who will appear in the form of beautiful woman, with a crown tied to their waist, who rides upon a camel. Their office is to tell of all things past, present and to come. They will also tell of all treasures that are hid and where they are. They will grant the love of all women both young and old. They govern 26 legions of spirits.

Binding Angel: Poeil

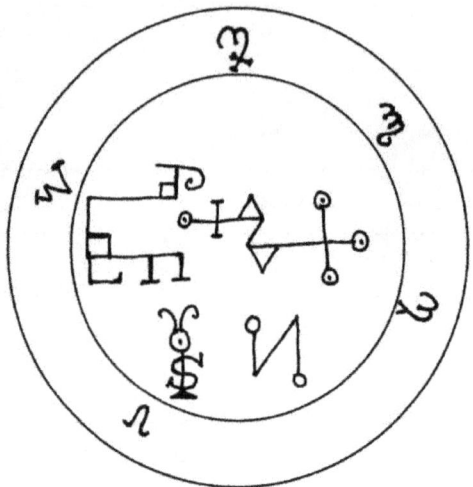

This angel will grant what the conjuror asks for and will also dominate fame, success and fortune. He also promotes moderation.

Angelic conjuration:

'Allevat Dominus omnes qui corrunt et erigit omnes elisos.'

'The Lord raiseth up all who fall and setteth up the broken.'

Psalm 145:14

Ose

Rank	President
Ruler	Ziminiar
Archangel	Auriel
Sign	♑ 10°-14°
Direction	South
Incense	Lavender and rose
Sigil colour	Green and orange
Metal	Mercury
Time of conjuration	Anytime except twilight unless the king has been invoked first

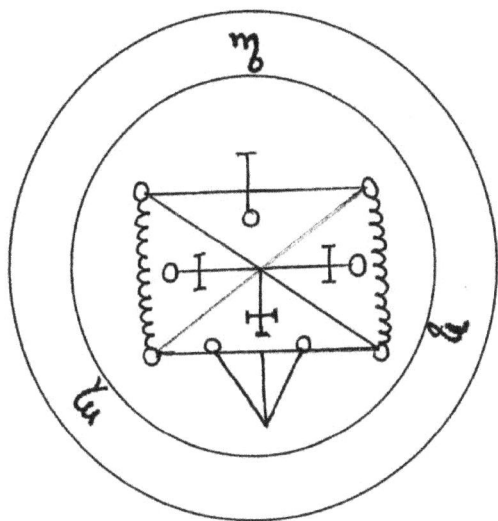

This spirit is also known as Oss or Voso, and is the fifty-seventh spirit. He is a great President who will appear as a leopard, but will take the shape of a man at the command of the conjuror. Their office is to making one cunning in the liberal sciences, and to give true answers of divine and secret things. They will also shape shift the conjuror according to his will, and they govern 30 legions of spirits.

Binding Angel: Nemamiah

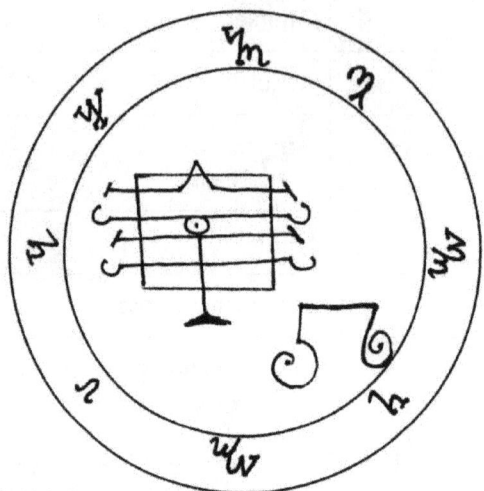

This angel will help those who need help to prosper, and will help to release prisoners too. They also dominate all combat and generals.

Angelic conjuration:

> 'Qui timent Dominum speraverunt in Domino adiutor eorum et protector eorum est.'

> 'They who fear the Lord have hoped in the Lord he is their helper and their protector.'

Psalm 113:19

Amy

Rank	President
Ruler	Ziminiar
Archangel	Auriel
Sign	♑ 15°-19°
Direction	South
Incense	Red sandal and lavender
Sigil colour	Green and orange
Metal	Mercury
Time of conjuration	Anytime except twilight at night, unless their king is invoked first

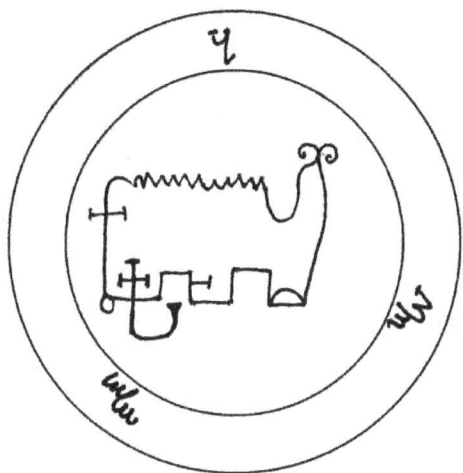

Amy is the fifty-eighth spirit and is a great President who will appear as a flame, but at the command of the conjuror he will assume human form. His office is to teach astrology and all liberal sciences. He grants good familiars and can show where treasure is hidden and the spirits that guard it. He governs 30 legions of spirits.

Binding Angel: Yeialel

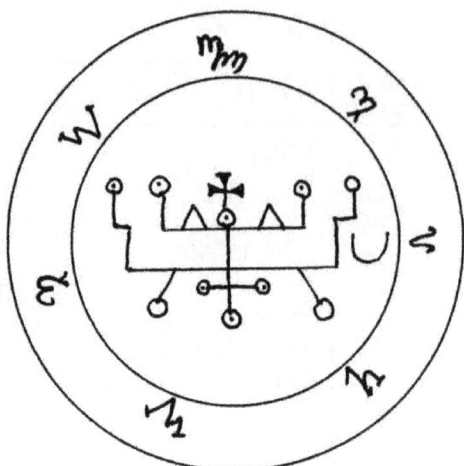

This angel will help against all troubles; they will also heal eye disease. As the angel dominates iron, they favour all locksmiths and knife grinders.

Angelic conjuration:

'Et anima mea turbata est valde sed tu Domine usque quo.'

'My soul is greatly troubled but thou O Lord art here also.'

Psalm 6:5

Oriax

Rank	Duke
Ruler	Ziminiar
Archangel	Auriel
Sign	♑ 20°-24°
Direction	South
Incense	Storax and jasmine
Sigil colour	Orange and purple
Metal	Copper
Time of conjuration	From sunrise until noon in clear weather

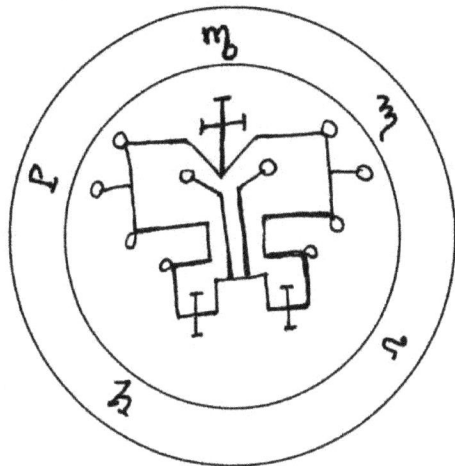

Oriax, who is also known as Orias, is the fifty-ninth spirit. He is a great marquis who will appear as a lion who is riding upon a horse; he has a serpent's tail and holds in his right hand two serpents. His office is to teach the virtue of all stars and to know the mansions of the planets. He will teach of their powers, he will also transform men and grant dignities, prelacies and the confirmation thereof. He will promote the favour of friend and foe and governs 30 legions of spirits.

Binding Angel: Harachel

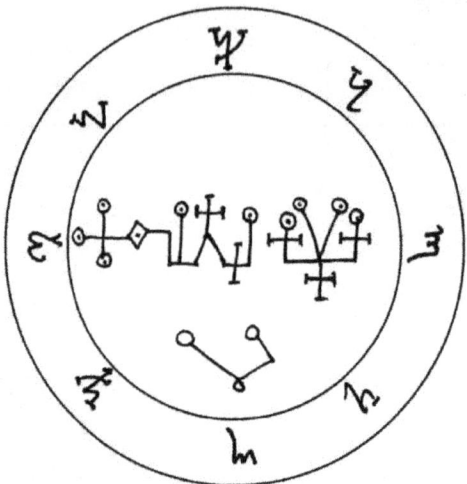

This angel will bind Oriax unto the conjuror's will; they will also protect females from sterility and rebellious children. They will also dominate treasure, archives and will influence the press.

Angelic conjuration:

> 'Ab ortu solis usque ad occasum laudabile nomen Domini.'

> 'From the rising of the sun to the going down of the same the word of the Lord is worthy to be praised.'

Psalm 113:3

Vapula

Rank	Duke
Ruler	Ziminiar
Archangel	Auriel
Sign	♑ 25°-29°
Direction	South
Incense	Storax and rose
Sigil colour	Green and orange
Metal	Copper
Time of conjuration	Sunrise until noon in clear weather

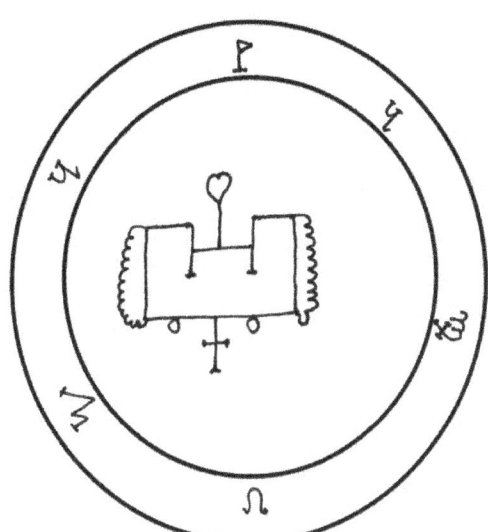

Vapula is the sixtieth spirit and he is a great duke who will appear as a lion with gryphon's wings. His office is to make men knowing and wise in all handicrafts and professions. He will also teach philosophy and other sciences. He governs 36 legions of spirits.

Binding Angel: Mitzrael

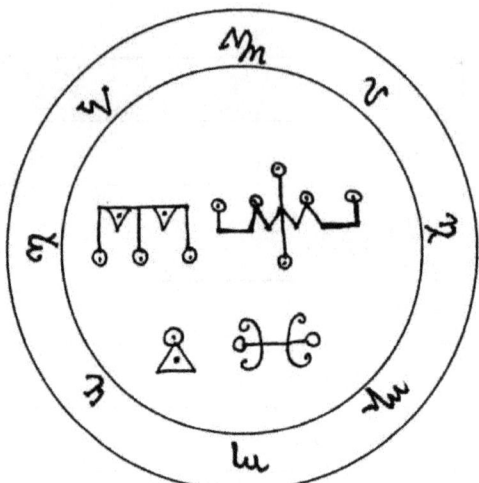

This angel will help to heal all ills of the spirit; they will also release those who are persecuted. They influence men of virtue and promote faithfulness.

Angelic conjuration:

'Iustus Dominus in omnibus viis suis et sanctus in omnibus operibus eius.'

'The Lord is just in all his ways and is blessed in all his works.'

Psalm 145:17

Zagan

Rank	King
Ruler	Amaymon
Archangel	Raphael
Sign	♒ 0°-4°
Direction	West
Incense	Frankincense and myrrh
Sigil colour	Black and gold
Metal	Gold
Time of conjuration	9am until noon and 3pm until sunset

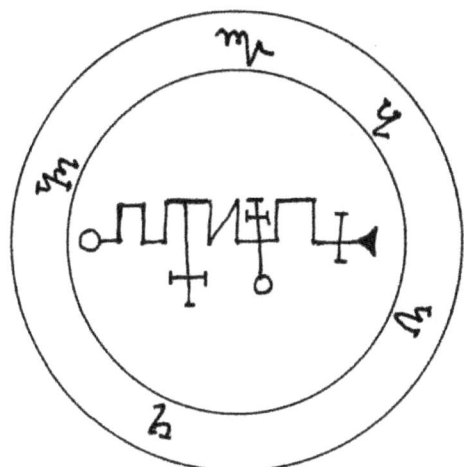

Zagan is the sixty-first spirit and he is a great King and President who will appear as a bull with gryphon's wings, at the command of the conjuror he will assume human form. His office is to make men witty and he can also turn water into wine and vice-versa. He can also turn all metals into coin and can also make fools wise.

Binding Angel: Umabel

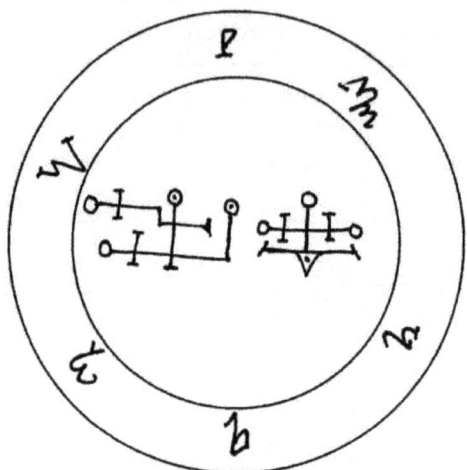

This angel will obtain friendships; they also dominate astronomy and physics. They also influence the emotions.

Angelic conjuration:

'Sit nomen Domini benedictum ex hoc nunc et usque in saeculum.'

'Let the name of the Lord be blessed from this time forth for evermore.'

Psalm 113:2

Volac

Rank	President
Ruler	Amaymon
Archangel	Raphael
Sign	♒ 5°- 9°
Direction	West
Incense	Myrrh and storax
Sigil colour	Black and gold
Metal	Mercury
Time of conjuration	Anytime except twilight at night, unless their king is invoked first

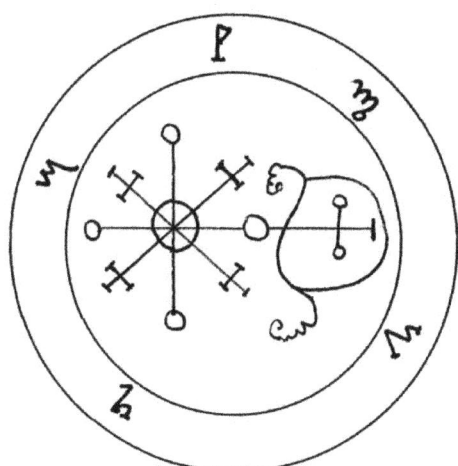

The sixty-second spirit is Volac, who is also known as Valu, Valak or Ualac, and he is a mighty President who will appear as a child with angel's wings and rides upon a two-headed dragon. His office is to give true answers of hidden treasure and to tell where serpents may be seen, which he will bring to you. He governs 38 legions of spirits.

Binding Angel: Yahehel

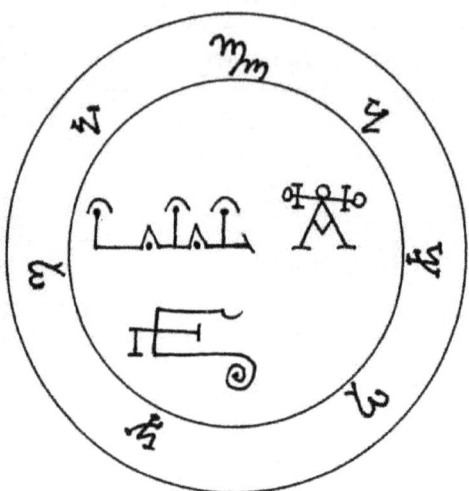

This angel will grant knowledge and wisdom. He is influential in promoting philosophy and enlightenment too.

Angelic conjuration:

> 'Vide quoniam mandata tua Domine dilexi secundum misericordiam vivificam.'

> 'See O Lord how I have delighted in thy commandments according to thy life-giving mercy.'

Psalm 119:159

Andras

Rank	Marquis
Ruler	Amaymon
Archangel	Raphael
Sign	♒ 10°-14°
Direction	West
Incense	Lavender and jasmine
Sigil colour	Orange and purple
Metal	Silver
Time of conjuration	3pm until sunrise

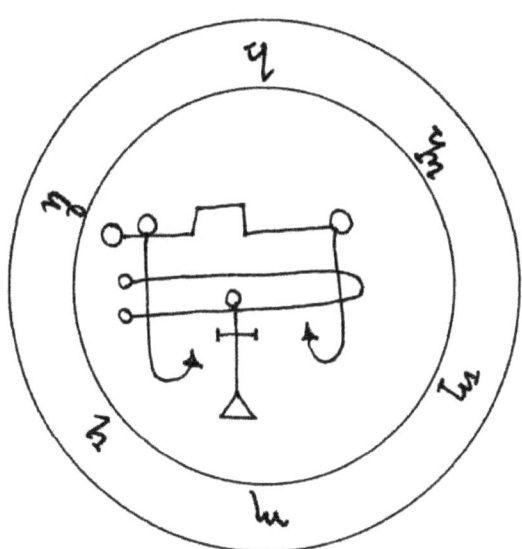

The sixty-third spirit is Andras who is a great marquis. He will appear as an angel with the head of a raven, and he carries a bright sword. He will be astride a black wolf and his office is to sow discord. If the conjuror is not careful he will slay him and his companions. He governs 30 legions of spirits.

Binding Angel: Annel

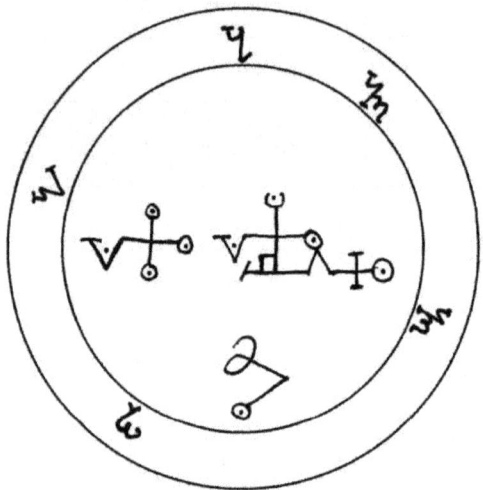

This angel protects against accidents and will help to maintain health and the healing of all ills.

Angelic conjuration:

> 'Servite Domino in laetitia, introite in conspectu eius in exultatione.'

> 'Serve ye the Lord with gladness and enter into his sight with exultation.'

Psalm 100:2

Flauros

Rank	Duke
Ruler	Amaymon
Archangel	Raphael
Sign	♒ 15°-19°
Direction	West
Incense	Storax and sandalwood
Sigil colour	Green and orange
Metal	Copper
Time of conjuration	Anytime from sunrise until noon

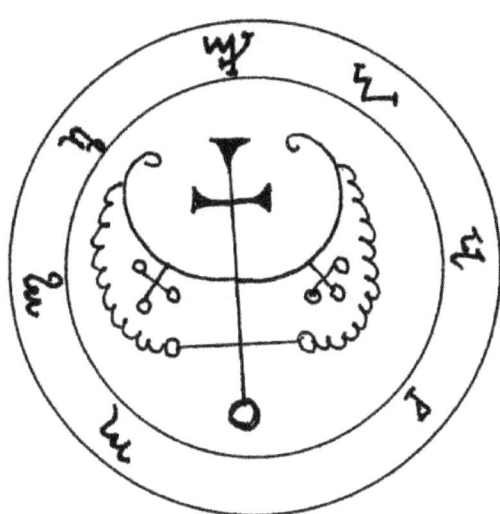

The sixty-fourth spirit is Flauros or Haures and is a great Duke who appears as a mighty leopard. He will adopt human form at the command of the conjuror, but it will be terrible with fiery eyes. His office is to tell of all things past, present and to come. If he is not constrained within the triangle of arte he will lie to the conjuror. He will also talk of the creation of the world and how other spirits fell. He will destroy the enemies of the conjuror and will restrain other spirits from tempting him. He governs 36 legions of spirits.

Binding Angel: Mechiel

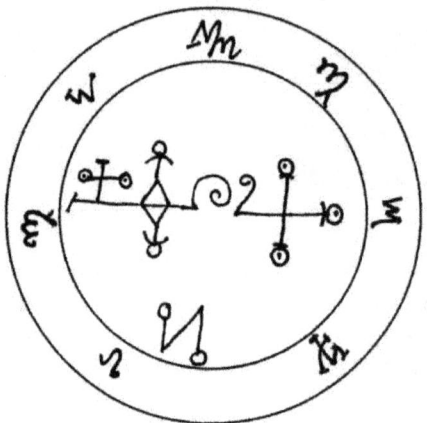

This angel will help to protect against rabies and fierce animals. He has influence over authors, orators and the learned, and also books and the press.

Angelic conjuration:

'Ecce oculi Domini super timentes et expectantes misericordiam eius'

'Behold the eyes of the Lord are upon those who fear him and hope in his loving kindness.'

Psalm 33:18

Andrealphus

Rank	Marquis
Ruler	Amaymon
Archangel	Raphael
Sign	♒ 20°- 24°
Direction	West
Incense	Sandalwood and jasmine
Sigil colour	Green and purple
Metal	Silver
Time of conjuration	3pm until sunrise

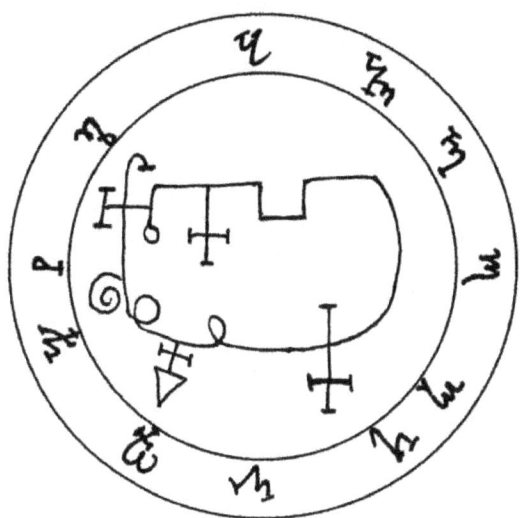

The sixty-fifth spirit is a mighty Marquis who will appear as a peacock, creating a great noise. He will assume human shape at the command of the conjuror. His office is to teach astronomy and geometry, he can also change a man into a bird. He governs 30 legions of spirits.

Binding Angel: Damabiah

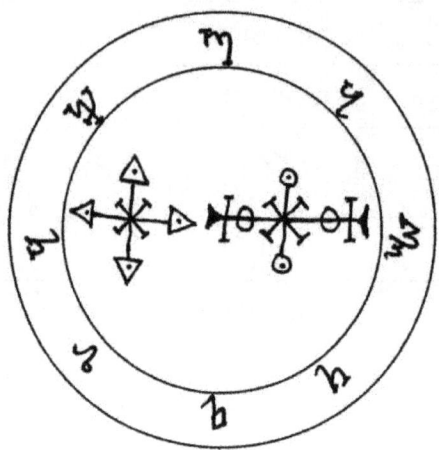

This angel will protect against sorcery, and will also help to obtain wisdom. He will also help fishermen and sailors too.

Angelic conjuration:

'Convertere Domine usque quo et deprecabilis esto super servos eius.'

'Turn O Lord, even here also, and be pleased with thy servants.'

Psalm 90:13

Cimejesi

Rank	Marquis
Ruler	Amaymon
Archangel	Raphael
Sign	♒ 25°- 29°
Direction	West
Incense	Red sandal and jasmine
Sigil colour	Green and purple
Metal	Silver
Time of conjuration	3pm until sunrise

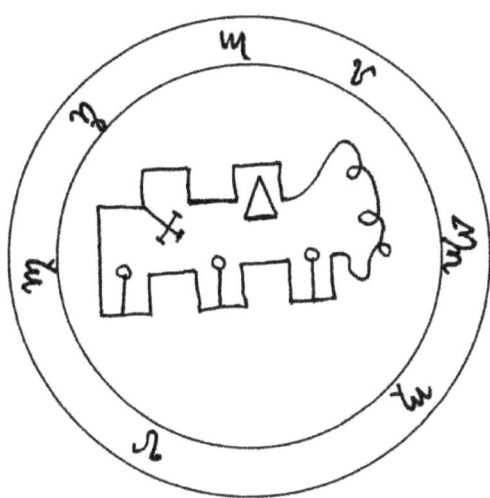

Cimejesi is the sixty-seventh spirit and he is a great Marquis, who will appear as a mighty warrior upon a black horse. He rules over all spirits that dwell in Africa and his office is to teach grammar, logic and rhetoric. Also he will discover all things that are lost or hid. He will find treasures too, and he has under his command 20 legions of spirits.

Binding Angel: Manakel

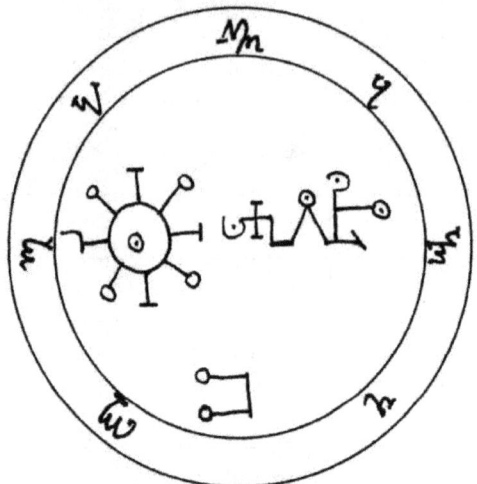

This angel will help to protect against leprosy and will also heal those who suffer therefrom. The angel will help to promote growth in all plants and will induce dreams and restful sleep too.

Angelic conjuration:

'Ne derelinquas me Domine Deus meus ne discesseris a me.'

'Neither leave me O Lord nor depart from me.'

Psalm 38:22

Amdusias

Rank	Duke
Ruler	Corson
Archangel	Gabriel
Sign	♓ 0°-4°
Direction	North
Incense	Cedar and rose
Sigil colour	Blue and green
Metal	Copper
Time of conjuration	Sunrise until noon in clear weather

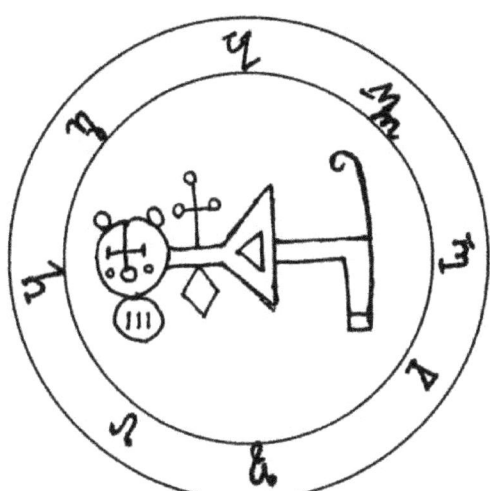

Amdusias is the sixty-seventh spirit and he is a great Duke. He will appear to the conjuror as a unicorn and at the command of the conjuror he will assume human form. He will cause trumpets and musical instruments to be heard and also trees to bend. He grants excellent familiars and governs 29 legions of spirits.

Binding Angel: Eiael

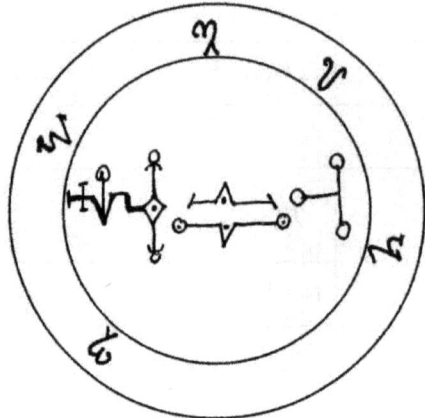

This angel will help to console in adversity, and will help to obtain wisdom and change in all matters. The angel is influential in all occult matters too.

Angelic conjuration:

'*Delectare in Domino et dabit tibi petitiones cordis tui.*'

'Delight in the Lord and he will give thee the petitions of thy heart.'

Psalm 37:4

Belial

Rank	King
Ruler	Corson
Archangel	Gabriel
Sign	♓ 5°-9°
Direction	North
Incense	Cedar and olibanum
Sigil colour	Blue and gold
Metal	Gold
Time of conjuration	9am until noon and 3pm until sunset

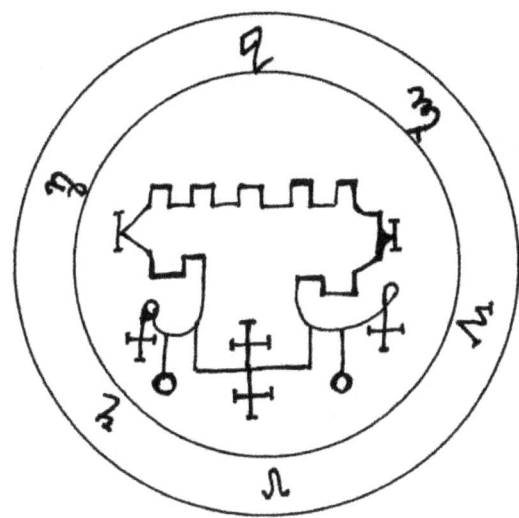

Belial who is the sixty-eighth spirit is a Great King and was created next under Lucifer. He will appear as two beautiful angels who are sitting in a chariot of fire. He will speak with a comely voice and declares that he fell first from among the worthier spirits that were before Mikael and other heavenly angels. His office is to distribute presentations and senatorships. He will also cause friendship between enemies. He commands eighty legions of spirits and grants good familiars. He must have offerings or he will not grant true answers and he must also be constrained by divine power or else he will not be true.

Binding Angel: Chabuiah

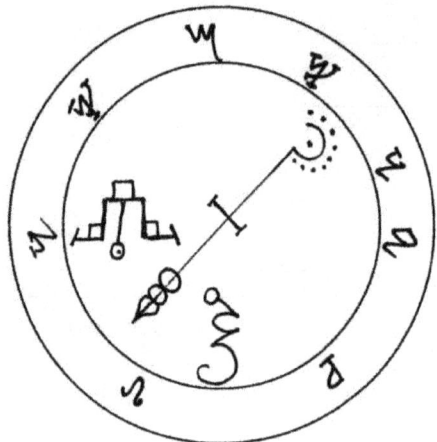

The angel Chabuiah will help to maintain health and cure disease. He also dominates all matters of agriculture, fertility and the earth.

Angelic conjuration:

" *Confitendum Domino quoniam in aeternum misericordia euis bonum et'*

'Confess to the Lord for he is God and his mercy is forever.'

Psalm 106:1

Decarabia

Rank	Marquis
Ruler	Corson
Archangel	Gabriel
Sign	♓ 10°-14°
Direction	North
Incense	jasmine and lotus
Sigil colour	purple
Metal	silver
Time of conjuration	3pm until sunrise

The sixty-ninth spirit will appear in the form of a star but will also appear human at the command of the conjuror. He grants the knowledge of birds and also precious stones, he will cause birds to fly before the conjuror. He governs 30 legions of spirits.

Binding Angel: Rachel

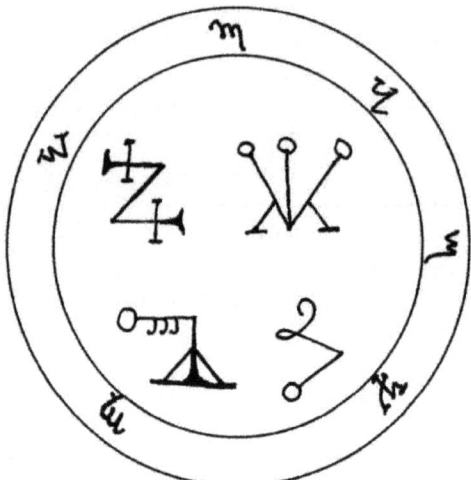

This angel will help to find all things that are lost or stolen, and influences all legal matters and judgements. He will also promote fame too.

Angelic conjuration:

> '*Dominus pars haereditatis meae et calicis meae tu es qui restitues haereditatem meam mihi.*'

> '*The Lord is my inheritance and my cup and it is thou who restorest my inheritance.*'

Psalm 16:5

Seere

Rank	Prince
Ruler	Corson
Archangel	Gabriel
Sign	♓ 15°-19°
Direction	North
Incense	Jasmine and cedar
Sigil colour	Blue and purple
Metal	Tin
Time of conjuration	Any hour of the day

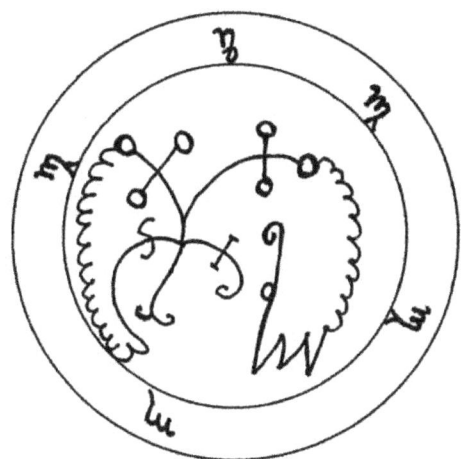

Seere is the seventieth spirit and he is a mighty Prince, who appears as a beautiful man who rides upon a winged horse. His office is to come and go and to bring an abundance of all good things. He will carry and fetch anything that the conjuror will demand. He can quickly pass over the earth he can also reveal all theft and also where treasure is too. He is indifferent and of a good nature and is willing to do anything that is asked. He governs 26 legions of spirits.

Binding Angel: Yabamiah

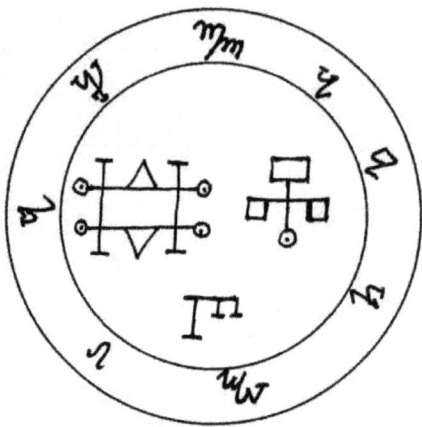

This angel will protect and regenerate, and will also promote inner harmony. He also dominates philosophical knowledge and influences nature.

Angelic conjuration:

'In principio creavit Deus caelum et terram.'

'In the beginning God created heaven and earth.'

Psalm 51:1

Dantalion

Rank	Duke
Ruler	Corson
Archangel	Gabriel
Sign	♓ 20°-24°
Direction	North
Incense	Dragon's blood and rose
Sigil colour	Red and green
Metal	Copper
Time of conjuration	Sunrise until noon in clear weather

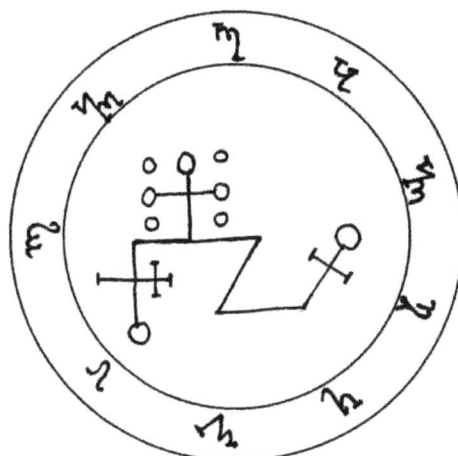

The seventy-first spirit is Dantalion who is a great Duke. He will appear at first as a man with many countenances, changing between male and female; he holds a book in his right hand too. His office is to teach all artes and sciences unto anyone. And to declare the secret councils of any person as he knows the thoughts of any person and he can also change them. He can cause love and show visions of people. He governs 36 legions of spirits.

Binding Angel: Haiel

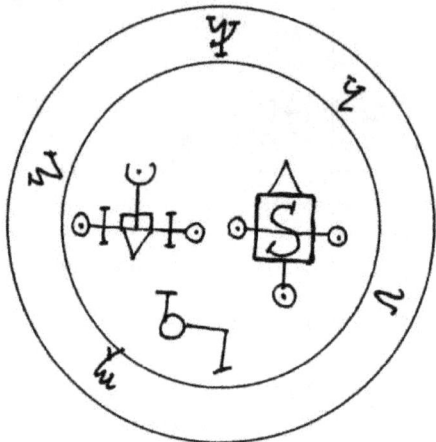

This is the angel Haiel who will confound all evil, and grants release from all enemies. He will grant victory and dominates weapons and soldiers; and influences all matters relating to iron.

Angelic conjuration:

> 'Confitebor Domino nimis in ore meo et in medio multorum laudabo eum.'

> 'I shall confess to the Lord with my mouth and praise him in the midst of the multitude.'

Psalm 109:30

Andromalus

Rank	Earl
Ruler	Corson
Archangel	Gabriel
Sign	♓ 25°-29°
Direction	North
Incense	Dragon's blood
Sigil colour	Red
Metal	Copper and silver
Time of conjuration	Any hour of the day

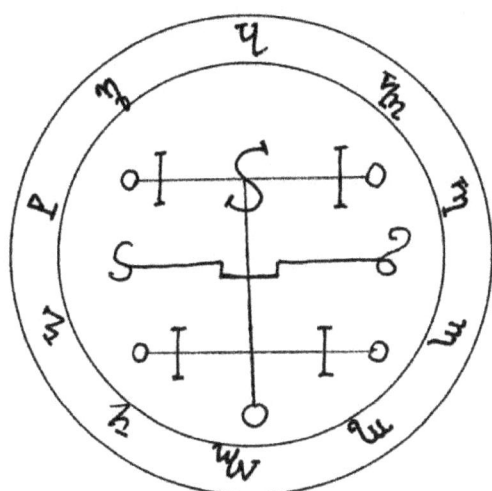

    Andromalus is the seventy-second spirit who is a great and mighty Earl. He will appear as a man who holds a large serpent in his hand. His office is to bring back thieves and any goods that have been stolen. He will discover all wickedness and underhand dealing; at the command of the conjuror he will punish wrongdoers and wicked people. He will also discover hidden treasure and he governs 36 legions of spirits.

Binding Angel: Mumiah

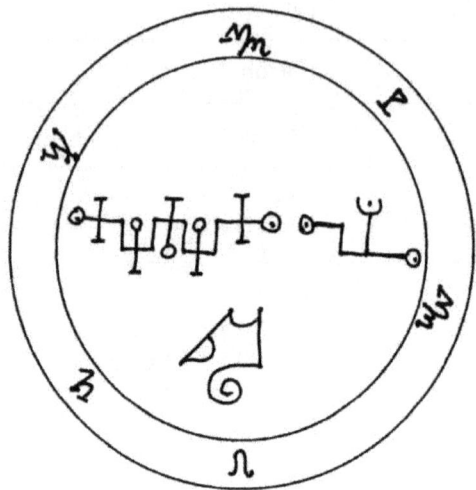

This is the angel who will bring every experience to a happy conclusion. The angel also dominates medicine and longevity.

Angelic conjuration:

> 'Convertere anima mea in requiem tuam quoniam Dominus benefactiet tibi.'

> 'Return to thy rest my soul for the Lord doeth thee good.'

Psalm 116:7

Ars Practica

Therefore by the Name of the Living God
Who hath formed the heavens above and the earth below
We command ye – Come unto us from all places

CHAPTER THREE

Of the Tools of Arte

There are various tools of arte which are of the utmost necessity for the success of operations of our arte. Their construction and consecration must be attended to with intent. Whilst there is room for variations upon a theme, consecrated tools of arte cannot be dismissed or skimped upon and still be expected to promote successful conjurations. I say this as their preparations are also part of the preparation of the conjuror and become part of their own consecration and initiation into the subtleties of our arte.

Although the four magical weapons of ritual magic are suitable for this work, there are some variations on these.

The conjuror will need to write out a working text on the arte with all the seals and conjurations written in consecrated inks and the book will also need to be consecrated as the arte demands. This becomes the book of spirits and it will obtain a magic of its own and much of the complexities of conjuration can then be dispensed with as bonds and bindings that have been created with the conjured spirits may then be invoked with a simplicity of arte. Magical workings such as holding a Mass, or something similar, and having the Book of Spirits present will help to empower the text and enliven the spirits therein.

Ideal workings for this are such practices as the Mass of On-Nophris (see *Liber Noctis*) or The Mass of the Tree of Life (see *Otz Chim*). With the consecration of the book each of the seventy-two spirits and their binding angels are called and in turn the spirit is reminded of their office and the aid of the angel is invoked to assist in their binding. This can be done in one operation of the arte.

Therefore let the book be one that is big enough to contain the seals and invocations of our arte. The conjuror will need inks of the seven planetary colours and a new pen. In the hour and day of Mercury when the moon is in her increase, lay the artefacts upon the altar, and perform the Kabbalistic Cross (K/C) and Lesser Banishing Ritual of the

Pentagram (LBRP) and anoint the brow with oil of Abra-Melin. Let prayers to God for assistance in the consecration of the book, inks and pen be performed. Now the conjuror will sprinkle with holy water of the arte and cense with frankincense or better still Abra-Melin incense. The fire, charcoal, and also the incense too will need to have been consecrated to the arte.

Of the Consecration of the Fire, Incense and Water:

Perform the K/C and take the perfumes of arte over which the conjuror will trace an equal-armed cross and say:

> 'O God of Abraham, God of Isaac, God of Jacob, Deign to bless these perfumes that they may receive strength, virtue and power to attract the Good Spirits, and to banish and cause to retire all hostile phantoms.
> Through Thee O Most Holy Adonai Who lives and reigns for ever Amen.'

Place charcoal in the censer, light and say:

> 'I exorcise thee O Creature of Fire by him through whom all things have been made so that every kind of phantasm may retire from thee and be unable to harm or deceive in any way through the invocation of the Most High Creator of all. Amen.'

Of the Water:

Take a new chalice, pottery would be ideal, and cense it unto the arte and use it for nothing else. Inscribe or paint the following sigils around its lip:

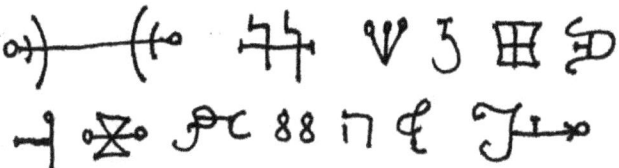

Half fill with clean water and also take salt in your hand and over the salt say the following:

> 'Tzabaoth Messiach Emanuel, Elohim Gibor Yod Heh Vav Heh

*O God Who art the Truth and the Life deign to bless and sanctify
this creature of salt
to serve unto us for help protection
and assistance in this art, experiment and operation and may it be
a succour unto us.'*

Then cast the salt into the water and say the following *Psalms*: 102: 54: 6: 67. Ideally an aspergillum may be prepared by cutting the following herbs on a Wednesday, in the hour of Mercury and on a rising moon:

Vervain, valerian, hyssop, lavender, fennel, sage, rosemary, basil and mint. Nine herbs in all.

An alternative will be to use a sprig of hyssop if the above is not possible, but this is the ideal. The herbs need to be bound with a thread that has been spun by a young girl. This will not be easy! As an alternative use white cotton thread and consecrate it whilst in a pure frame of mind. If you choose to bind the herbs to a suitable piece of wood as the handle then engrave the following sigils upon the handle:

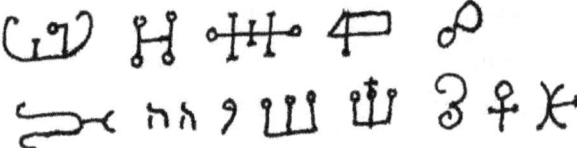

Of Inks and Pen:

Perform K/C and invoke God in words of your own choosing Now sprinkle with holy water and cense whilst saying:

*'ADRAI HAHLII TAMAII TILONAS ATHAMAS ZIANOR ADONAI
Banishing all deceit and error from this pen so that it may be of
virtue and efficacy to write all that I desire. Amen.'*

Then say over the inks:

*'I exorcise thee, O creature of Ink, by Anaireton, Simulator and the
holy name Adonai and by the Name of Him through whom all
things were made that thou be unto me an aid and succour in all
things which I wish to perform by thy aid.'*

Give thanks and close the rite with the Kabbalistic Cross.

Of the Book:

At sunrise on the full moon place the book on an altar which is draped in a white cloth and is lit by two new white candles, which have been consecrated unto the arte. Open with the magical formula that has been previously given. Sprinkle the book with holy waters and hold in the rising incense smoke and intone the following:

> 'Most Wise and Most High Creator of all things I pray thee for thy grace and mercy that thou mayest keep these characters from all deceit and error through thee O Most Holy Adonai Amen.'

Describe an equal-armed cross over the book and declare that the book has now been consecrated unto the arte. It is now ready to be written in.

Of the White Robe:

Take a white robe and upon the left side of the breast embroider the following sigils in red silken thread.

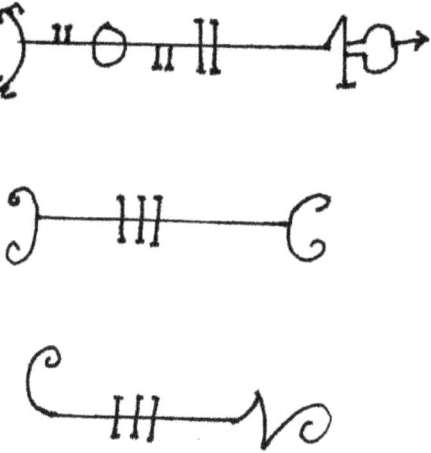

Let the robe be freshly washed and clean. Sprinkle it with holy water of arte and hold in the rising incense smoke saying:

> 'In the Mighty Names of God
> Let this robe be consecrated and dedicated unto all operations of the arte.'

Sprinkle with water and say:

'Let this white robe be an outer symbol of mine inner grace purified and sanctified unto the Glory of God the Most High.'

Of the Candles:

Acquire the candles on a waxing moon, ideally when the moon is domiciled in a fire sign. Upon them engrave the following symbols.

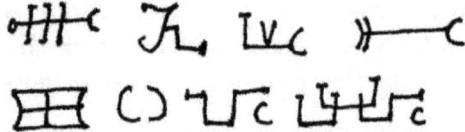

Afterwards recite the following *Psalms:* 103, 107, and say:

'O Lord God who governest all things let these candles of arte be blessed and sanctified unto the success thereof.'

Then asperge with holy water and cense saying:

'I exorcise thee O Creature of wax by him who alone hath created all things by his word and by virtue of him who is pure truth that thou cast out from thee every phantasm, perversion and deceit of the enemy and may the virtue and power of God enter into thee so that thou mayest give us light and chase far from us all fear or terror.'

When lighting the candles recite the following:

*'I exorcise thee O Creature of Fire in the Name of the Sovereign and Eternal Lord, by his Ineffable Name which is YOD HEH VAV HEH
By the name IAH and by the name of power EL
That thou mayest enlighten the heart of all spirits which we shall call unto this circle so that they may appear before us without fraud and deceit through him who hath created all things.'*

Of the Burin:

This will be found to be a useful tool for inscribing upon the cup and various magical instruments of the arte. Take a sharp needle and insert in a piece of boxwood or hazel, after stripping off the bark and smoothing it down, so that it creates the handle. The wood needs to be cut with a new knife on a Sunday on a waxing moon.

Consecration Rite

Perform LBRP and use the following invocation:

> 'Blessed art Thou Lord of Creation
> Blessed art Thou whom Nature hath not formed
> Blessed art Thou God the Vast and Mighty One
> Lord of the Light and of the Darkness.'

State the aim of the rite. Then sprinkle the Burin with the water of the arte and hold in the rising incense smoke saying:

> 'Adonai most High
> Deign to bless and consecrate this burin that it may obtain the necessary virtue through thee O Most Holy Adonai
> Whose Kingdom endureth unto the Ages of the Ages.'

Anoint with the holy oil of Abra-Melin. With some minor adjustments this basic rite can be adapted to suit the consecration of the tools of arte.

Of the Sword:

Let a clean sword be taken and upon the day and hour of Mercury engrave the following names, whilst this can be done in Hebrew it is not necessary if you are not familiar with the alphabet as the wording will not mean much to you. Along the blade inscribe the following names:

YOD HEH VAV HEH: ADONAI: EHEIEH: YAYAI

יאיאי אהיה אדמי יהוה

On the other side engrave the following names:

ELOHIM GIBOR

אלהים גבור

Sprinkle with water and cense and say the following conjuration over the sword:

> 'I conjure thee O sword by these names Abrahach: Abrach: Abrahadabra
> Yod Heh Vav Heh
> That thou servest me for a strength and defence in all magical operations against all mine enemies visible and invisible.
> For I conjure thee anew
> by the Holy Indivisible Name EL strong and wonderful.
> By the name Shaddai Almighty;
> And by the names Qadosh Qadosh Qadosh Adonai Elohim

Tzabaoth Emanuel the first and the last
Wisdom, Way, Life, Truth, Chief, Speech, Word, Splendour, Priest, Messiach, Immortal. By these names then and by the other names I conjure thee O Sword that thou servest me for a protection in all adversities.'

Of the Knife with the Black Hilt:

Ideally the knife should have the handle made from boxwood that has been cut at the rising of the sun with a new knife. However I have used wood from a lightning-struck oak tree which works well. If all else fails use a piece of oak that you have cut. When it has been dried and the bark scraped off it can be painted black and signs painted or engraved thereon. A knife blade can easily be inserted into the handle and be very effective as you have created it by yourself and tools that have that extra input from the conjuror, regardless how *'homemade'* they may seem are of far more potency. However as a very last resort buy a new suitable knife for conjuration only.

Let the knife be consecrated on a Saturday when the moon is waxing. Perform LBRP and heat the blade upon some hot charcoal blocks. Then drop some of your own blood upon it, hemlock juice is useful too but is highly poisonous and not easy to find. This knife will have the same powers as the sword and can be used often in its place. Therefore use the previous conjurations and formulae for the sword but adapt accordingly.

Of the Knife with the White Hilt:

This is used for cutting herbs and also for engraving. It must be consecrated when the moon is in the sign of Aries or Scorpio and when the moon is waxing. Again adapt the rite of consecration for the sword.

Signs upon the Black Knife:

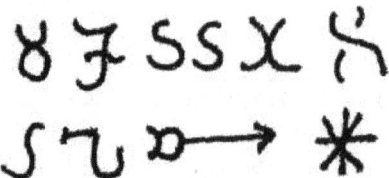

Signs upon the White Knife:

The Wand

This is cut from one-year-old Hazelwood, which is a young branch that has never borne fruit. Cut on the day of Mercury at sunrise. The following signs will be engraved upon the side of the wand. Perform LBRP and a general invocation. The wand needs to be sprinkled with water and cense as you have done with the other tools of arte, and also anointed with the Abra-Melin oil.

Recite over the Wand as it is held in the rising incense smoke the following:

> 'Adonai Most Holy deign to bless and consecrate this wand that it may obtain the necessary virtue through Thee O Most Holy Adonai!
> Whose kingdom endureth unto the Ages of Ages.'

Sigils upon Wand:

The Altar

The altar becomes the holy table before God the Most High and is your working top within your holy circle of arte which has been drawn as a boundary between the worlds. The altar will need to be waist height and ideally it is seen as a double cube, which is a cube on top of a cube. It will need to be covered with a white cloth and both will need dedication to the arte. Creating your own rite will suffice for this.

The Hexagram of Solomon

The hexagram is used as a means to control the spirits and to bring them to order. It must be shown to the spirit on its manifestation, either in the triangle of arte or in the shewstone and is used to demonstrate the authority of the conjuror and to grant protection too. It can be inscribed upon silver plate or drawn and painted upon parchment. It is often worn at the hem of the robe but can also be worn around the neck suspended on a cord or thin silver chain. It must be blessed and consecrated before use. Perform LBRP and state the purpose of your working, this is always important in any magical working and needs to be clearly stated without any ambiguity or weak thinking.

Let your magical will always be clear, precise and to the point. Use a suitable invocation to God of your own devising, bless and consecrate the lamen that it is a defence and that all spirits that are evoked will be subject unto its presence and that of the bearer. The symbol of the hexagram upon the seal is your symbol of your union with the highest, with God, the lower and higher worlds, that are not only reflecting one another, but which are in harmony and are twinned in holy union.

Thus the Hexagram of Solomon becomes the holy symbol that represents the conjuror's divine authority. This is important for the success of the operation of the arte. It is your will and your divinity, your spiritual connection with the highest that will grant success to your magical workings. Thus the spirit has no alternative but to obey your will as your will becomes a reflection of the will of the highest. You have a spirituality that is different to any other creature that God has created and it is moments such as in acts of conjuration, when you are endeavouring to work with the very forces that have been set in motion to enable the fate of individuals and nations high or lowly to manifest that this spiritual fact becomes apparent.

Thus the conjuror becomes an important player in the divine scheme of things as they, the conjuror, will set forces abroad that can and will cause change in the mundane and inner worlds, that are reflected within mankind and without.

Having performed the LBRP and invocations to God, take the Hexagram of Solomon and sprinkle it with holy water declaring that all negativity is washed from its being. Then hold it in the rising incense smoke, frankincense or church incense will suffice for this, and recite the *91st Psalm* over it. This will also be used in the consecration of the Pentacle and Ring of Solomon, as it encapsulates the magical will.

> *'He who dwells in the shelter of the Most High who abides in the shadow of the Almighty will say to the Lord, 'My refuge and my fortress My God in whom I trust.'*
> *For he will deliver thee from the snare of the fowler and from the deadly pestilence, he will cover thee with his pinions and under his wings thou wilt find refuge for his faithfulness is a shield and buckler.*
> *Thou shalt not fear the terror of the night nor the arrow that flies by day nor the pestilence that stalks in darkness Nor the destruction that wastes at noonday. A thousand may fall at thy side ten thousand at thy right side but it will not come near thee.*
> *Thou wilt only look with thine eyes and see the recompense of the wicked.*
> *Because thou hath made the Lord thy refuge, The Most High thy habitation no evil shall befall thee.*
> *No scourge come near thy tent.*
> *For he will give his angels charge of thee to guard thee in all thy*

ways.
On their hands shalt they bear thee up lest thou shalt dash thy foot against a stone.
Thou will tread upon the lion and the adder
The young lion and the serpent wilt thou trample under foot.
Because he cleaves to me in love I will deliver him
I will protect him because he knoweth my name.
When he calleth unto me I will answer him I will rescue and honour him.
With long life shall I satisfy him and show him my salvation.'

Anoint the lamen with Abra-Melin oil again declaring your intent and breathe upon it and see the lamen glow with its holy sanctity and declare:

'Alpha et Omega
Thou O Great God Who art the beginning and the end.'
'Tetragrammaton
Thou God Almighty power be ever present with us to guard and protect us and let thy Holy Spirit and presence be now and always with us.'

Give thanks to God for the success of the work and wrap it up in a white cloth, silk would be ideal. By making changes where relevant this ritual format can be adapted to consecrate the Pentacle and Ring.

Ring of Solomon

The Ring of Solomon is a silver ring that has the following engraved upon it: Tetragrammaton, Anaphaxeton and Mikael. The ring becomes a defence against the wiles of the spirits and is also part of the holy regalia stating the conjuror's holy office. The name Tetragrammaton is engraved upon the inside, whilst Anaphaxeton and Mikael will be engraved upon the outer.

These names are also used in the conjuration of the triangle of arte and I will explain them in depth accordingly.

The Pentacle of Solomon

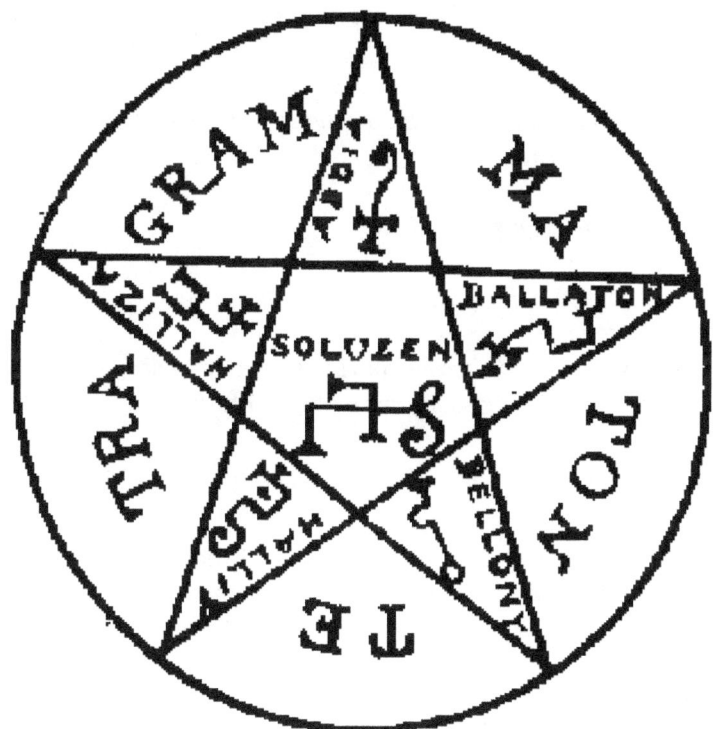

The Pentacle of Solomon will need to be constructed in the day and hour of Mercury. It can be created from parchment or a silver disc; both will need to be consecrated. The Pentacle becomes a device for the defence and preservation of the conjuror. It also displays the spiritual authority of the conjuror. The five-pointed star, which is displayed in the middle of the circle, is spiritual man being active, and showing that the four elements are now crowned by spirit within the psyche of the conjuror. Thus this is the symbol of the microcosm being active and under the divine auspices of the Most High, the Macrocosm. Therefore lesser spiritual creatures can do no other than obey the conjuror as part of divine expression. This is a symbol that represents the conjuror in harmony with divine will and that which they do is but a manifestation of this.

As previously, perform LBRP and invocations; let the Pentagram be consecrated with fire and water too. After the 91st *Psalm* anoint the Pentagram with the oil of Abra-Melin and say:

'Tetragrammaton
Thou God of Almighty Power be ever present with us to guard and protect us and let The Holy Spirit and presence be now and always with us.'
'Soluzen
I command thee O Spirit of whatsoever region thou art to come unto this circle.'
'Halliza
And appear in human form.'
'Bellator
And speak unto us audibly in our mother tongue.'
'Bellonoy
And show and discover unto us all treasures that thou knowest of or that is in thy keeping and deliver it unto us quietly.'
'Hally Fra
And answer all such questions as we may demand without any defect now at this time.'

Give thanks and close as previously. All regalia will need to be wrapped in clean white silk cloth and placed somewhere safe and out of sight. These are now consecrated and deemed holy for the successful workings of the arte.

CHAPTER FOUR

Of Preparation

Of Baths and Preparations:

Correct preparation of the conjuror is important, as this will help get the conjuror into the right frame of mind. Whilst fasts and restrictions are a useful means for this they need to be handled with some consideration. For example, one can hardly perform a three-day fast if you are involved with heavy manual labour. If fasting during the winter time you will feel the cold more, and it is not an easy thing to do at the best of times. However if you are taking a vegetarian diet, this is in my view, better for your magic as you are half way there. The missing of a meal or two prior to the working will not be such a hardship and will suffice as you will need some energy to carry the working through.

The grimoires suggest that a basic and restricted diet that avoids anything of animal origin, and starting several days prior to the working, is to be followed. If you are not a vegetarian then this will be relevant to you. You will also need to avoid sexual activity for the three days before the working as this will allow the body's life force to build up; it will also help to concentrate the will. Avoid alcohol and drugs several days before the working too. This will give sufficient time for them to work through the system. Drug use in this work is in my view unwise, as the conjuror will need to be completely in control of themselves at all times during the work. These spirits are not simple friendly puppies and they can cause havoc if they get out of the conjuror's control. Therefore the conjuror has to be strong-willed and focused at all times for success to manifest.

It will be prudent to remember that the angels told Kelly, *'Long may they knock, those who are filthily apparelled.'* Something to be mindful of as the angelic orders will not approach the conjuror if the conjuror is in a chaotic and dishevelled state, although the demonic will do so only too readily. Meditating upon the working at set times, on the run-up to the working will also be useful. Such magical exercises as the Middle Pillar are ideal, so is the Mass of On Nophris (see *Liber Noctis*).

Going over the ritual will help to connect the conjuror with the current that s/he is endeavouring to work with. As far as possible cut back on conversation and socialising with other people during this period, as this will help to focus the magical will. Granted, with the demands of everyday living, this won't be easy to perform, but do try to avoid frivolous contact with people. Giving alms and acts of generosity are looked upon favourably, should the opportunity arise to do so. The *Key of Solomon* makes it quite clear that the conjuror is expected to live modestly and is to avoid all immodesty and impiety, whilst preparing for the working. This can be seen as disregarding all things which are irrelevant to the successful outcome of the working, thus these acts will become part of the consecration of the conjuror and are instrumental in the formulation of their magical will.

Of Baths:

The magical bath can be a shower with a jug of holy water being poured over the conjuror afterwards. The bath or the jug of water will have to be consecrated as the arte demands. When washing recite the following words:

>'Mertalia-Musalia-Dophalia-Onemalia
>Zitanseia-Goldapharia-Dedulsaria-Ghevialaiara Gheminaira-Gegropheira-Cedahi-Gilthar-Godieb-Ezoiil Musil-Grassil-Tamen-Pueri-Godu-Huznoth-Astachoth Tzabaoth-Adonai-Agla-On-El-Tetragrammaton-Shema Aresion-Anaphaxeton-Segilaton-Primeumaton.'

When pouring the water over your head declare:

>'Asperges me, Domine, hyssopo et mundabor, Lavabis me, et super nivem dealbabor.'

Meaning:

>"Purge me with hyssop O Lord and I shall be clean
>Wash me and I shall be whiter than snow."

When donning the magical robe say

>'By the figurative mysteries of these garments I will clothe me with

the armour of salvation In the strength of the God Most High. Ancor Amacor Amides Theodonias Anitor That my desired end may be effected through thy strength O Adonai unto whom be the praise and the glory forever.'

Having washed and robed approach the altar, kneel and give prayer to God for success in the working. Then anoint your head with the holy oil of Abra-Melin and call upon your higher self to assist you in this work.

The Triangle of Arte:

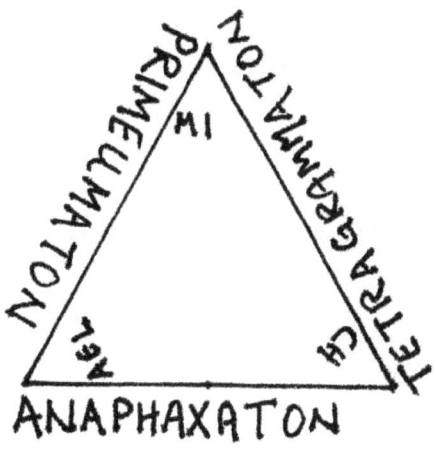

This is a design for the constraining of the energies that manifest which can be placed outside the circle. It is to be an equilateral triangle with the point facing away from you and towards the quarter of the spirit. It is consecrated with fire and water, it must also be traced over with the sword or black knife. It can also be created with a white cord of silk that is placed upon the altar with the shewstone therein. It will have to be consecrated as directed with the seal of the spirit under the shewstone or in the triangle outside the circle. In some grimoires, such as the *Heptameron* a triangle is not used, and the spirit manifests where it will. The triangle is a good method, as not only is it easier to constrain the spirit, but it is also where you focus your will when reciting the conjuration, and therefore with your will so focused it cannot but succeed. It can also be traced upon the ground with the wand, and this is ideal if working outside. The Triangle of Arte is consecrated by the use of the following names which are intoned firmly when the conjuror traces the Triangle with the sword. This is done after blessing and consecrating the triangle with fire and water

Sprinkle holy water around the edge of the triangle whilst saying the following:

> 'Let this Holy Triangle of Arte be blessed and made holy.'

Cense the boundary of the triangle saying:

> 'Therefore be thou consecrated unto my will.'

Trace over the boundaries again with the sword and declare that:

> 'I charge thee O Triangle of Arte that thou constrain those spirits that make manifest within thee and that they depart peaceably and affably unto their realms and habitations causing no harm nor fear to anyone or anything. For I charge thee by my Holy Will and in the names of the God Most High!'

Retrace over the boundary again saying:

> 'Tetragrammaton
> Thou Great God of Almighty Power be ever present with us to guard and protect us and let thy Holy Spirit and presence be now and always with us.'
> 'Primeumaton
> Thou who art the first and the last, let all spirits be subject unto us, and let the spirit be bound in this triangle.'
> 'Anaphaxeton
> Thou Great God of all the Heavenly Host.'
> 'Mikael
> By thy Holy Angel Mikael until I shall discharge him.'

The Circle of Arte:

The circle becomes the limits of the conjuror's attention and is a place, once consecrated, that is between the worlds. It becomes a replica of creation and the conjuror is the God that is at its centre. Magical circles can be constructed in various ways and their boundary, like the triangle's, is never to be crossed when in use. They can be permanently drawn on the ground if there is space with a diameter of nine feet.

However the reality is that the conjuror will simply have to work within a restricted area, therefore work with what you have available. The circle can be inscribed upon the ground with the wand if working outside but this will have to be somewhere secluded and safe from intrusion. There are various methods of constructing a magical circle, some more complex then others. The circle that is shown within the *Goetia* texts is based upon the Holy Names from the Kabbalah. The texts show them to be written around the circle in three circles, often as a serpent.

Prayers to God are said first for success of the operation, and the conjuror now anoints their brow with the holy oil of Abra-Melin; thus placing themselves under the divine auspices of the Most High. Now the consecration of the ground and the circle can take place. Draw upon the ground, by whatever means, a circle. This will be the physical boundary of your working space. Outside the circle draw in the relevant quarter the triangle as described previously. Or if using a shewstone then place the triangle marked with a silken cord upon the altar and with the shewstone inside.

The LBRP is now performed and the circle boundary can be consecrated with fire and water as follows: Starting in the east sprinkle the holy water around the boundary saying:

> 'Let the Sorcerer/ess sprinkle with the lustral waters of the loud resounding sea.'

Take up the censer and again starting in the east carry the censer around the boundary of the circle saying:

> 'And when after all the phantoms have disappeared thou shall see the holy and formless fire,
> The fire that flashes through the hidden depths of the universe. Hear thou the voice of fire.'

Perform the K/C and take the wand, facing East trace the circle three times as you recite the following conjuration:

> 'For I conjure thee O Circle of Power to be a boundary and a defence from all hostility and malignancy by the might and power of the Holy Names.'
> EHIEH: Almighty God who dwellest in the Highest. HAIOTH: Great King of Heaven and all the powers therein. METATRON: Of the hosts of Holy Archangels and Angels. RESCHITH: Hear thou the prayers of thy servant who puts his trust in thee.
> HAGALGALIM: Let thy holy angels be commanded to assist me in this operation of the arte.
> YHVH: God Almighty and Omnipotent hear my prayer. HADONAT: Command thy Holy Angels above the stars. OPHANIM: Assist and aid thy servant.

YOPHIEL: That I may command all spirits of air, water, fire, earth and hell.
MASLOTH: Let it be unto thy glory and to the good of all mankind.
YHVH: Almighty and Omnipotent God, hear my prayer. ELOHIM: God be with us and be thou always present. BINAH: Strengthen and support us both now and forever. ARALIM: In these undertakings which we perform but as instruments in thy hands.
ZABBATHAI: In thy hands O Great God of Tzabaoth.

Start second circumbulation in the east saying:

HESEL: O Thou Great God, creator of the planets and the hosts of heaven.
HASMALIM: Command them by thy mighty power.
ZELEZ: Be thou present and assist us, thy poor servants both now and for ever.
ELOHIM GIBOR: Almighty and eternal God, ever living God.
SERAPHIM: Command thy Seraphim.
MADIM: Attend on us now, assist us and defend us from all perils and dangers.
ELOHA: Almighty God be present now and for evermore.
TETRAGRAMMATON: Let thine almighty power and presence guard us protect us now and for evermore.
MIKAEL: Let Mikael who is under thee and general of thy heavenly hosts.
SCHEMES: Assist us in our undertakings.

Start third circumbulation in the east saying:

YHVH: O God Almighty Omnipotent God hear my prayer.
TZABAOTH: Thou Great God of Tzabaoth.
NETZACH: Thou all-seeing God.
ELOHIM: Be thou present with us O God, and let thy presence be with us now and for always.
HANIEL: Let thy holy angel Haniel minister unto us.
ELOHIM: Be thou O God present with us and let thy holy presence be with us now and for always.
TZABAOTH: O thou Great God of Tzabaoth, be thou present with us now and always.
RAPHAEL: Let thy holy angel Raphael wait upon us at this time and forever.
COCHAB: Come thou now and expel all danger from us both now and for ever.
SADAI: Thou Great God of all wisdom and knowledge. YESAL:

Instruct thy poor and humble servant
CHERUBIM: Thy holy Cherubim.
GABRIEL: By thy holy angel Gabriel, who is the author and messenger of all good tidings.
LEVANAH: Direct and support us at this time forever.

Having finished the consecration of the circle recite the following:

'By the might of the Holy Names of God Let this circle be blessed consecrated and dedicated unto my will.
So Mote It Be'

CHAPTER FIVE

Modus Operandi

There are five areas that you will need to give utmost consideration to for success in this arte. Firstly, there are the orisons or opening prayers. These can be performed with the use of the Middle Pillar working which lends itself well to this work. The second point of note is the invocations, or calls. Whilst the use of the traditional invocations are of importance, it will not be easy reading by candle light so the invocations are best learnt if possible.

However if you forget the wording then extemporise as you do not want to impair the flow and interrupt the working with a loss of concentration. You must keep the intent going without any interruptions. The invocation of the binding angel is of great importance and is achieved by the reciting of the relevant verse from the *Psalms* and with a clear request for the binding of the spirit according to one's will.

The third point will be the spirit's reception. This can take some time to manifest and may not be in traditional form or even be visible at all. The spirit will manifest in the triangle or shewstone as laid down, here it can be interrogated and worked with. The spirit must be challenged as to its identity and the Hexagram of Solomon must be revealed to it reminding it of the conjuror's divinity and the links that they have with God.

The fourth point will be the binding of the spirit and will be done by oath or an agreement that it will perform the task diligently unto the end. Do not request work that is outside its office, although the office of many of the spirits shows something of the medieval mind and that which was important to it. However with some subtle interpretations and interrogations one may be surprised at the spirit's versatility.

Part of the binding will be to arrange that the spirit is easier to contact another time also you may arrange that the spirit is rewarded by prayers to God or the lighting of a candle in its name when the working is successful. This helps to energise the spirit, but do not see it as a pact, the conjuror is in control of the working and should not be seduced from their spiritual position in the cosmic scheme of things.

Finally the Licence to Depart must be given and under no circumstances must it be omitted. This applies even if you feel the spirit has not appeared, and if this is the case there will still be all sorts of astral flotsam and jetsam which have been attracted to the working and will be out on the periphery.

Therefore it is important that you banish and clear the atmosphere so that it can settle down again. If the working does not bring the desired result within the given time the spirit is often resummoned and instructed again, mindful of the fact that it could be bound and punished for being disobedient. This is not a useful situation and is one that can be avoided by having the links between yourself and divinity strengthened as the spirit will have no choice but to do the will of the conjuror. Bribes are not a good idea, nor is complete damnation of the spirit despite the fact that the grimoires grant ample scope for this to happen. I feel that it is best to firstly work with the correct spirit, strengthen one's own links with God through meditation and prayer etc. Adequate binding of the spirit and work with the binding angel will be of importance in achieving this. Sometimes spirits in my experience will leave the matter to the very last minute before they do something about it, another time I have known them to be very prompt with promoting the desired outcome. There is never a dull moment with the *Goetia* spirits.

Praxis

Having cleaned your working area and marked out your circle and triangle, the altar is set and you are purified both in body, mind and spirit; the work begins in earnest. The seal of the spirit is drawn, with the seal of the binding angel upon the back of the figure and it is consecrated. The binding angel is invoked to aid the conjuror and to bind the spirit unto their will. It is placed within the triangle, if using the shewstone place the seal under the stone.

Then the performance of the LBRP takes place clearing the working area including the triangle if it is placed outside the circle for a physical manifestation. If this is the case then the triangle is consecrated and the circle is now blessed and consecrated too. If you are using the shewstone within the triangle set upon the altar now would be the time to consecrate it. Face East, prayers to God are now given for the success of the working, and the conjuror anoints themselves with the Abra-Melin oil and says:

> 'Holy art Thou Lord of Creation
> For Thy glory flows out unto the ends of creation rejoicing Be Thou with me as I perform this work which I dedicate unto Thee.'

Pick up the wand and intone the Enochian invocation:

> 'OL SONUFVAORSAGI GOHO IADA BALTA ELEXARPEH COMANANU TABITOM
> ZODAKARA EKA ZODAKARA OD ZODAMERANU ODO KIKLE QAA PIAPE PIAMOEL OD VAOAN.'

Said as:

> 'OH-EL-SO-NOOF-VAY-OH-AIR-SAH-JEE-GOH-HOH-EE-AH-DAH-
> BAL-TAH-EL-EX-AR-PEH-HEH-CO-MAH-NAH-NOO-TAH-BEE-TOH-
> EM-ZODH-AH-KAH-RAH-EH-KAH-ZOD-AH-KAH-RAH-OH-DAH-
> ZOHD-AH-MER-AH-AH-NOO-OH-DOH-KEE-KLAY-KAH-AH-PEE-
> AH-PAY-PE-AH-MOH-ELL-OH-DAH-VAY-OH-AH-NOO.'

Meaning:

> "I reign over you sayeth the God of Justice ELEXARPEH-COMANANU-TABITOM Move therefore and show thyselves. Appear unto us: open the mysteries of thy creation the balance of righteousness and truth."

Still facing east intone the following or something of your own creation:

> 'I invoke thee, thou angels of the Celestial Spheres whose dwelling is in the invisible.
> For thou art the guardians of the Universe be thou the guardians of this my sacred sphere.
> Keep far from me the evil and the unbalanced Inspire and strengthen me
> so that I may preserve unsullied this abode of the mysteries of God. Let my sphere be pure and holy That I may enter therein
> and become a partaker of the secrets of the light divine.'

Contemplate the sanctity and sacredness of your space for a few moments and then perform the Middle Pillar with the clear intent that you are invoking the highest aspects of your being and by placing the working under the auspices of the God Most High you are invoking your own spiritual authority. Now place your consciousness in the sphere of Kether above your head and intone the following after identifying, even momentarily, with Kether:

> 'I AM HE THE BORNLESS SPIRIT HAVING SIGHT IN THE FEET STRONG AND IMMORTAL FIRE!
> I AM HE THE TRUTH
> I AM HE WHO HATES THAT EVIL SHOULD BE WROUGHT IN THE WORLD
> I AM HE WHO LIGHTENETH AND THUNDERETH
> I AM HE FROM WHOM IS THE SHOWER
> OF THE LIFE ON EARTH
> I AM HE THE BEGETTER AND THE MANIFESTER UNTO THE LIGHT
> THE HEART GIRT WITH A SERPENT IS MY NAME!'

See your aura glow now as you recite the following:

> 'COME THOU FORTH AND FOLLOW ME AND MAKE ALL SPIRITS SUBJECT UNTO ME SO THAT EVERY SPIRIT OF THE FIRMAMENT
> AND OF THE ETHER UPON THE EARTH AND ON DRY LAND OR IN THE WATER
> AND OF RUSHING AIR OR OF ROARING FIRE AND EVERY SPELL OF GOD THE VAST AND MIGHTY ONE
> MAY BE MADE OBEDIENT UNTO ME!
> IAO SABAO!
> SUCH ARE THE WORDS!'

Whilst this working is demanding it is of importance as it will help to establish and strengthen your spiritual links with those higher aspects of your being. Thus it is not the everyday you, but your most potent God-inspired self who now commands and performs the evocation.

Face the quarter that is associated with the spirit and call upon the binding angel and invoke their aid, by reciting the invocation that is drawn from the Psalms and is associated with each of the angelic forces:

> 'For and by the Mighty and Holy God
> I (your name) do invoke thine aid O Holy Angel xyz
> To bind the spirit xxx
> According to my will that they manifest as I do will causing no harm nor fear to anyone or thing.

> *Furthermore that the spirit xxx is obedient unto me*
> *And that they depart peaceably when licensed to do so!'*

Recite the invoking lines from the relevant *Psalm* and again call upon the angel to assist.

Trace with your wand over the shewstone or the triangle of arte, an equal-armed cross. Do not cross over any of the magical boundaries that you have put in place when you do this and call the spirit by name to make manifest in the shewstone or triangle as you will. Holding your wand upon high, declare the following conjuration with full intent, gazing at the shewstone or triangle accordingly:

> *'I invoke and conjure thee O spirit XYZ and being armed with power from the Supreme Majesty*
> *I strongly command thee by Beralanensis-Baldachiensis-Paumachiae et Apologiae And by the most powerful Princes Genio-Liachiae*
> *Ministers of the Tartarian abode, Chief Prince of the Seat of Apologia in the ninth region.*
> *I exorcise and powerfully command thee O Spirit XYZ in and by him who said the word and it was done and by all the holy and most glorious names of the Most High and True God.*
> *And by these his most Holy Names.*
> *Adonai-El-Elohim-Zebaoth-Elion-Eserchie-Jah- Tetragrammaton-Sadai*
> *That ye do forthwith appear and show yourself unto me in this triangle before this circle/or in the shewstone, in a fair and human shape without any deformity or ugly shape and without delay do you come to make rational answers unto all those things which I shall ask of thee and come ye peaceably, visibly and affably without any delay manifesting what I desire being conjured by the eternal and living and true God Helioren.*
> *For I conjure thee by the special and true name of your God that you are obedient to and by the name of your King....... which bears rule over you that forthwith you come without tarrying and fulfil my desire and command.*
> *Persist to the end therein according unto my will and I conjure thee by Him to whom all creatures are obedient and by his ineffable name Tetragrammaton YHVH which being heard the elements are over turned the air is shaken, the sea runneth back, the fire is quenched, the earth trembleth and all hosts of Celestial, Terrestrial and Infernal do tremble and are troubled and confounded*

> *together that you visibly and affably speak to me with a clear voice intelligibly and without any ambiguity.*
> *Therefore come Ye!*
> *In the name Adonai Zebaoth Adonai Aiorem!*
> *Come, Come why stay thee*
> *Adonai Sadai The King of Kings Commands Thee!!'*

By now the atmosphere will be getting intense to say the least, anything can happen! Watch the shewstone or the triangle wherein the spirit will manifest and call again. If you are using a skryer to watch the shewstone they will say if anything is happening in the stone. Repeat the conjuration again if need be and watch. The spirit may take a little time to manifest, and may only be felt rather than seen. If nothing is happening then move on to the second conjuration although the above if repeated will suffice generally. Call upon God to assist you and invoke the binding angel again if it is felt necessary:

> *'I invocate and conjure thee O spirit XYZ to manifest and show thyself within this shewstone/triangle of arte in fair and comely form without any deformity and tortuosity by the name and in the name Yah and Vav Which Adam heard and spake and by the name Ioth which Jacob heard from the angel wrestling with him and was delivered from the hands of Esau his brother, and by the name of God Agla which Lot heard and was saved with his family and by the name of Anapheneton which Aaron heard and spake and become wise. And by the name Schemes Amathai which Joshua called upon and the sun stood still and by the name Emanuel which the three children Shadrach-Meseck and Abednego sung in the midst of the fiery furnace and were delivered. And by the name of Alpha et Omega which Daniel names and destroys Bel and the dragon and by the name Zebaoth which Moses names and all the rivers and waters in Egypt are turned into blood. And by the name Eserchie Oriston which Moses named and all the rivers brought forth frogs and they went into the houses of the Egyptians destroying all things and by the name Elion which Moses called upon and there was a great hail such as there was never since the creation of the world to this day and by the name Adonai which Moses named and there came up locusts throughout all the land of Egypt and destroyed all that the hail had left. And by the name Hagios and by the seal of Adonai and by O Theos Iscyros Athanatos Paracletos and by the three holy and sacred names Agla On Tetragrammaton.*

And by the dreadful judgement of God which is before the face of divine Majesty who is mighty and most powerful and by the four beasts that stood before the throne having eyes before and behind and by the fire round the throne. And by the holy angels of heaven and by the mighty wisdom of God and by the seal of Basdathea And by the name Primeumaton which Moses named and the earth opened up and swallowed Corah-Dalthan-Abiram For I command that thou make faithful answers unto my demands and to perform all my desires so far as in thy office that thou art capable to perform.

Therefore come thou peaceably, visibly and affably now without delay to manifest what I desire speaking with perfect and clear voice intelligible and to my understanding.

Repeat if necessary; this will be rare as the spirit will very likely be present although you are not aware of it. If you feel nothing is happening then it is traditional to move on to constraints and curses which I am not keen on using. If nothing is happening then go back and re-work the Middle Pillar and invoke the binding angel a further time and then repeat the conjurations. Sometimes it can take a little while for the spirit to come through, remember this is an arte and not an exact science. It may be that the spirit is elsewhere, if so invoke the King for assistance in bringing the spirit to you.

Invocation of the King:

'O Ye Great Mighty and Powerful King.......
Who bears rule by the power of the supreme God El over all spirits both superior and inferior of the infernal order in the domain of the (state quarter)
I invocate and command ye by the especial and true name of your God and by the God that you worship and by the seal of your creation and by the most mighty and powerful name of God YHVH Tetragrammaton
Who cast ye out of heaven with all other infernal spirits and by the most powerful and great names of God who created Heaven and Earth and Hell and all things contained in them and by their powers and virtue and by the name Primeumaton. Who commanded the whole host of heaven that you cause enforce and compel the spirit XYZ to come unto me! Here in this triangle of arte/shewstone in a fair and comely form without doing any harm to me or any other creature and to answer truly and faithfully unto

my requests that I may accomplish my will and desires in knowing and obtaining any matter or thing which by your office you know is proper for him to perform or to accomplish, through the power of God EL who createth and disposeth of all things Celestial, Aerial, Terrestrial and Infernal.'

On the spirit's arrival test the spirit and display the Hexagram of Solomon. If the spirit is true they will stay; if someone else they will disappear.

Pointing the wand at the spirit say:

'Welcome O spirit XYZ
For I have conjured thee by the names of him who art the creator of all things and unto whom all things are subject.
And I XXX who art made in the Holy Image of God, and loved by God and empowered by his Almighty Presence
do welcome thee unto this showstone/triangle of arte.
Therefore in his Holy Name declare thy name and office.

Display the Hexagram of Solomon to the spirit and declare:

'Behold the Hexagram of Solomon that Mighty King!
Be thou bound unto my will.'

State the work that you require the spirit to do and the spirit must swear to fulfil the task. For this bind it with the names of God and the name of the binding angel too.

It will be easier if you make an arrangement with the spirit that it will in future manifest or attend to your will if you call them by a simpler procedure. Some conjurors will create a vessel to house the spirit's seal therein with objects that are in keeping with their nature, such as gemstones or herbs etc. This is a valid way of working with such spirits and has much to commend it. When the working is over then the conjuror will licence the spirit to depart. This is something which must never be omitted.

'O Spirit XYZ
as thou hath arrived in peace, now therefore go in peace.
For I do licence thee to depart unto thy proper realms and habitations.
Go in peace causing no fear nor harm to anyone or anything and may the peace of God
be upon thee and upon this working.
And be thou ready to come when thou art called.
So Mote It Be!'

Let the visions clear and the tensions in the room settle and then give thanks to God and to the binding angel for assisting you in the working. Afterwards reconsecrate the circle with fire and water as you did previously. Then trace the circle widdershins three times and let it fade. Finally finish with the LBRP.

It will be useful to have something to eat and drink to earth the experience and also to record the working. You will need to keep the seal of the spirit somewhere safe, sometimes the conjuror will arrange with the spirit that if the seal is censed and a suitable invocation is uttered then the spirit will perform the will of the conjuror. This will save a lot of preparation for future workings and the seal can be housed in a special pot that has the seal of Solomon painted upon the lid.

Of Angels and their Invocation:

Angelic spirits are not *'New Age'* so do not think of them in such demeaning terms! Although angelic forces are popular in New Age culture, it is not realised that they are far more potent than is the general perception. They are not to be commanded as the spirits of the *Goetia*, the angelic forces are invoked into the shewstone and if the conjuror has been diligent in their preparations and are favoured by God then the visions of the angelic forces will be granted. Approach them in piety and you will be successful in your invocations.

Having followed the preparations for *Goetia* conjuration let the altar cloth be white and the candles of the same colour as the angel's astrological schema. Also use the incense that is given too. The shewstone is placed upon the altar and the seal of the angel will be consecrated as given and placed underneath the stone. You will not need the triangle of arte for this working. Facing the angelic quarter, kneel and pray that God will grant the angel to come to you. Skrying into the shewstone recite the following invocation:

> *'O thou great and blessed Angel ABC*
> *O Holy Angel vouchsafe to descend from thy holy mansion which is celestial with thy holy influence and presence into this crystal stone that I may behold thy glory and enjoy thy society and assistance both now and for ever hereafter.*
> *O thou who art higher than the fourth heaven and knoweth the secret of Elanel. Thou that rideth upon the wings of the winds and art mighty and potent in thy celestial and superlunary motion do thou descend and be present I pray thee and I humbly desire and*

entreat thee. That if ever I have merited thy society or if any of my actions and intentions be real and pure and sanctified before thee bring thy external presence hither and converse with me one of thy submissive pupils. By ye name of the Great God YHVH whereunto the whole choir of heaven singeth continually O Mappa la man Hallelujah. Amen!'

This invocation may have to be repeated several times but the conjuror must wait for the angel to manifest so do not rush the working. Test the spirit by using the names of God to see if the angel is who they say they are. They will fade if they are not, but if they are, they will seem more potent by the utterance of the holy names.

Ask for the help or the request that you need, providing that it is in their office to perform. Another form of working will to be write their name upon a candle that is of their colour, and petition them to work for you. This can be done by again using the colours and incense which have already been given. Place a consecrated seal bearing their sigil underneath the candle and recite the relevant *Psalm* verse attributed to the angel. Gazing into the candle flame see your petition coming to pass. Give thanks to the angel and to God for the aid granted and let the candle burn out. The rite can be performed the following day and the day after. Thus invoking the angel thrice. Repetition is a simple but effective method of working. Other factors to consider are whether the moon is waxing or waning. The importance of this will depend upon your work, also consider if the moon is in the astrological sign that is associated with the angel as this will be useful as this is a good time to work with the angelic force. Or let the degrees of the zodiac which they are associated with be sitting upon the tenth house of the chart; however for this you will need a working knowledge of astrology. Therefore let God favour you, for everything is but an expression of the *'Creator of All Things'*, from whom we all come and unto whom we all return.

*'From God we are born To God do we return
What Then is There To Fear?'*

Suggested Further Reading

Agrippa, C & Tyson, D. (ed) (2005) *The Three Books of Occult Philosophy*. Llewellyn, Minnesota

DuQuette, L.M. (2011) *Aleister Crowley's Illustrated Goetia*. Original Falcon Press, Arizona

DuQuette, L.M. (1999) *My Life with the Spirits*. Weiser Books, Maine

Howard, M. (1977) *Candle Burning its Occult Significance*. Aquarian Press, Wellingborough

Leitch, A. (2005) *Secrets of the Magical Grimoires*. Llewellyn, Minnesota

Lisiewski, J. (2011) *Howlings from the Pit*. Original Falcon Press, Arizona

Mathers, S. L. (1972) *The Key of Solomon*. Routledge Kegan Paul, London

Nottingham, G. St. M (2004) *Liber Noctis*. Avalonia, London

Nottingham, G. St. M (2014) *Ars Salomonis*. Avalonia, London

Nottingham, G. St. M (2014) *Otz Chim*. Avalonia, London

Peterson, J. (2001) *The Lesser Key of Solomon*. Weiser Books, Maine

Regardie, I. (1980) *The Tree of Life*. Aquarian Press. Wellingborough

Regardie, I. (1978) *The Middle Pillar*. Llewellyn, Minnesota

Runyon, C. (1996) *The Book of Solomon's Magic*. Church of the Hermetic Science Inc, USA

Skinner, S. & Rankine, D. (2007) *The Goetia of Dr Rudd*. Golden Hoard Press, Singapore

Skinner, S. (2006) *The Complete Magician's Tables*. Golden Hoard Press, Singapore

Stratton-Kent, J. (2013) *Geosophia*. Scarlet Imprint, Brighton

Index

A

Abra-Melin oil 163, 167, 169, 177, 179, 184
Achiah 30
Agares 19, 21
Aiel 34
Aim 61
Aladiah 36
Alloces 119
altar 162, 165, 169, 177, 179, 183, 184, 190
Amaymon .41, 43, 45, 47, 49, 51, 80, 89, 91, 95, 97, 99, 137, 139, 141, 143, 145, 147
Amdusias 149
Amon 29
Amy 131
Andras 141
Andrealphus 145
Andromalus 159
Aniel 90
Annel 142
Ariel 108, 189
Aries 19, 168
Ars Salomonis 14
Asaliah 110
Asmodai .... See Asmoday
Asmoday 79
aspergillum 164
Astaroth 73
Auriel ... 29, 31, 33, 35, 37, 39, 77, 79, 81, 83, 85, 87, 125, 127, 129, 131, 133, 135

B

Bael 16
Balam 117
Barbatos 31
basil 164
bath 113, 176
Bathin 51
Beal .... See Berith
Beleth 41
Belial 151
Berith 71
Bifrons 107
black 11, 37, 51, 63, 81, 83, 95, 105, 115, 125, 127, 137, 139, 141, 147, 168, 177
blue 21, 25, 27, 39, 59, 61, 63, 69, 71, 73, 105, 107, 113, 115, 121, 125, 149, 151, 155
Bolfrey .... See Berith
Book of Spirits 162
Botis 49
boxwood 166, 168
Buer 35
Bune 67
burin 166, 167

C

Caliel 52
Camio 121
candles 108, 165, 166, 190
cedar 21, 25, 27, 39, 59, 61, 63,

69, 71, 73, 105, 107, 113, 115, 125, 149, 151, 155
censer 163, 179
Chaamiah 92
Chabuiah 152
charcoal 163, 168
Cimejesi 147
circle 42, 166, 169, 173, 174, 177, 178, 179, 181, 183, 186, 190
copper. 19, 27, 31, 37, 45, 47, 51, 53, 61, 67, 71, 73, 83, 91, 95, 97, 99, 107, 109, 113, 119, 123, 127, 133, 135, 143, 149, 157, 159
Corson 53, 55, 57, 59, 61, 63, 101, 103, 105, 107, 109, 111, 149, 151, 153, 155, 157, 159
Crocell 113

D

Damabiah 146
Daniel 116, 187
Dantalion 157
de Abano, Peter 13
decans 14
Decarabia 153
dragon's blood 57, 59, 75, 91, 95, 107, 117, 157, 159

E

East.. 6, 16, 17, 19, 21, 23, 25, 27, 42, 65, 67, 69, 71, 73, 75, 113, 115, 117, 119, 121, 123, 179, 180, 184
Eiael 150
Elemiah 24
Eligos 45
Emamiah 120
Exodus 6, 13

F

fennel 164

fire ... 29, 62, 72, 80, 85, 119, 121, 151, 163, 166, 173, 177, 179, 180, 186, 188, 190
Flauros 143
Focalor 97
Foras 77
Forneus .... See Fornius
Fornius 75
Fortune, Dion 14
frankincense ... 16, 21, 23, 33, 41, 55, 65, 67, 105, 117, 121, 123, 137, 163, 171
Furcas 115
Furfur 83

G

Gaap 81
Gabriel 53, 55, 57, 59, 61, 63, 101, 103, 105, 107, 109, 111, 149, 151, 153, 155, 157, 159, 181
Gamigin .... 23, See Samigina
Glasya-Labolas 65
Goap 16, 19, 21, 23, 25, 27, 65, 67, 69, 71, 73, 75, 113, 115, 117, 119, 121, 123
Goetia 11, 13, 15, 89, 179, 183, 190
gold 16, 19, 21, 23, 33, 41, 55, 65, 67, 71, 79, 105, 112, 117, 121, 123, 137, 139, 151
green ... 27, 29, 31, 37, 43, 45, 47, 49, 51, 53, 61, 67, 69, 71, 85, 87, 89, 91, 97, 99, 109, 113, 119, 123, 127, 129, 131, 135, 143, 145, 147, 149, 157
Gremory 127
grey 39
Gusion 37

H

Haagenti 111

Haaih 68
Hahahel 98
Hahasiah 118
Hahiah 40
Hahuiah 64
Haiel 158
Hakamiah 48
Halphas 91
Harachel 134
Haril 46
Haures .... See Flauros
hazel 42, 166
Heptameron 13, 177
Hexagram of Solomon 170, 171, 182, 189
holy water 163, 164, 165, 166, 171, 176, 178, 179
hyssop 164, 176

I

Ieliel 20
incense 10, 15, 16, 19, 21, 23, 25, 27, 29, 31, 33, 35, 37, 39, 41, 43, 45, 47, 49, 51, 53, 55, 57, 59, 61, 63, 65, 67, 69, 71, 73, 75, 77, 79, 81, 83, 85, 87, 89, 91, 95, 97, 99, 101, 103, 105, 107, 109, 111, 113, 115, 117, 119, 121, 123, 125, 127, 129, 131, 133, 135, 137, 139, 141, 143, 145, 147, 149, 151, 153, 155, 157, 159, 163, 165, 167, 169, 171, 190, 191
Ipos 59

J

jasmine 23, 29, 43, 53, 55, 63, 75, 101, 109, 111, 133, 141, 145, 147, 153, 155

K

Kabbalistic Cross .. 162, 163, 164, 179
Kahetel 32
Kavakiah 86
Kelly, Edward 175
Kether 185
Key of Solomon 176
King Solomon 101
knife 132, 166, 168, 177

L

Lauviah 38
lavender 25, 33, 35, 41, 43, 49, 65, 77, 97, 111, 121, 129, 131, 141, 164
LBRP 163, 167, 168, 169, 170, 171, 173, 179, 183, 190
lead 115
Lectabel 78
Lehachiah 84
Lelahel 28
Leraje 43
Lesser Banishing Ritual of the Pentagram .... 163, See LBRP
Leuviah 54
Leviah 50
Liber Noctis 14, 162, 176
lotus 103, 153
Lucifer 33, 151

M

Malphas 93
Manakel 148
Marax 57
Marbas 25
Marchosias 85
Mass of On-Nophris 162
Mebahel 44
Mebahiah 126
Mechiel 144
Mehasiah 26
Melanel 62
mercury 25, 35, 49, 65, 77, 81,

111, 121, 129, 131, 139
Mercury 162, 164, 167, 169, 173
Middle Pillar .. 176, 182, 185, 188
Mihael 112
Mikael .. 16, 19, 21, 23, 25, 27, 65, 67, 69, 71, 73, 75, 100, 113, 115, 117, 119, 121, 123, 152, 172, 178, 180
mint 164
Mitzrael 136
Monadel 88
Mumiah 160
Murmur 123
myrrh ... 37, 39, 49, 51, 81, 83, 95, 115, 125, 127, 137, 139

N

Naberius 63
Nanael 122
Nelekael 58
Nemamiah 130
Nithael 124
Nith-Haiah 66
noon 16, 19, 27, 31, 33, 37, 41, 45, 47, 51, 53, 55, 61, 67, 71, 73, 79, 97, 99, 105, 109, 113, 117, 119, 123, 127, 133, 135, 137, 143, 149, 151, 157
North 53, 55, 57, 59, 61, 63, 101, 103, 105, 107, 109, 111, 149, 151, 153, 155, 157, 159

O

olibanum .... 79, 151, See frankincense
Omael 76
orange. 25, 33, 35, 41, 43, 65, 77, 79, 81, 97, 99, 111, 129, 131, 133, 135, 141, 143
Orias .... See Oriax
Oriax 133, 134
Orobas 125

Ose 129
Oss .... See Ose
Otz Chim 14, 162

P

Paimon 33
Pentacle of Solomon 173
pepper ... 16, 19, 57, 83, 103, 119
Phenex 89
Poeil 128
Psalm 10.1 40
Psalm 100.2 142
Psalm 102.13 126
Psalm 103.19 124
Psalm 103.8 30
Psalm 104.31 118
Psalm 106.1 152
Psalm 109.30 159
Psalm 113.19 130
Psalm 113.2 138
Psalm 113.3 134
Psalm 116.1 86
Psalm 116.7 160
Psalm 119.108 104
Psalm 119.145 68
Psalm 119.159 140
Psalm 119.2 56
Psalm 119.75 122
Psalm 12.4 98
Psalm 120.5 60
Psalm 120.8 62
Psalm 121.7 100
Psalm 131.3 84
Psalm 140.2 70
Psalm 145.17 136
Psalm 145.3 114
Psalm 145.9 108
Psalm 15.9 116
Psalm 16.5 154
Psalm 18.47 38
Psalm 21.20 20

Psalm 25.6 34
Psalm 26.8 88
Psalm 3.5 18
Psalm 30.18 58
Psalm 32.18 64
Psalm 33.18 144
Psalm 33.22 36
Psalm 33.4 26
Psalm 33.4 80
Psalm 35.24 52
Psalm 37.4 150
Psalm 38.22 148
Psalm 39.1 54
Psalm 51.1 156
Psalm 54.4 74
Psalm 6.4 24
Psalm 6.5 132
Psalm 7.18 120
Psalm 70.16 78
Psalm 70.6 76
Psalm 71.12 72
Psalm 8.1 50
Psalm 87.1 48
Psalm 88.14 102
Psalm 9.11 28
Psalm 9.2 66
Psalm 9.9 44
Psalm 90.13 146
Psalm 90.2 22
Psalm 90.20 90
Psalm 90.9 92
Psalm 91 171
Psalm 91.11 82
Psalm 92.6 110
Psalm 93.22 46
Psalm 94.18 106
Psalm 95.6 32
Psalm 97.6 42
Psalm 98.15 96
Psalm 98.2 112
purple .. 23, 29, 43, 49, 53, 55, 63, 85, 89, 101, 103, 109, 111, 133, 141, 145, 147, 153, 155
Purson 55

R

Rachel 154
Raphael 41, 43, 45, 47, 49, 51, 89, 91, 95, 97, 99, 137, 139, 141, 143, 145, 147, 180
Raum 95
red . 16, 19, 47, 57, 59, 71, 73, 75, 83, 85, 87, 91, 95, 99, 101, 103, 107, 117, 119, 127, 147, 157, 159, 165
red sandal 131
red sandalwood 45
Rehael 94
Reiyel 74
Ring of Solomon 171, 172
robe 165, 166, 170, 176
Ronove 69
rose 19, 27, 29, 31, 37, 45, 47, 51, 53, 61, 67, 69, 71, 87, 89, 97, 109, 113, 119, 123, 129, 135, 149, 157
rosemary 164

S

Sabnock 101
sage 164
Sagittarius 31, 35
Sallos 53
Samigina 23
sandalwood 45, 143, 145
Schemhamephorasch 13, 90
Scorpio 168
Sealiah 106
Seere 10, 11, 155
Shax 103
Sheahiah 72
shewstone .. 10, 11, 14, 170, 177, 179, 182, 183, 184, 186, 187,

188, 190
silver 11, 23, 29, 42, 43, 63, 69, 75, 83, 85, 89, 91, 95, 101, 103, 107, 141, 145, 147, 153, 159, 170, 172, 173
Sitael 22
Sitri 39
South ... 29, 31, 33, 35, 37, 39, 77, 79, 81, 83, 85, 87, 125, 127, 129, 131, 133, 135
Stolas 87
storax .. 79, 81, 99, 133, 135, 139, 143
sunrise. 19, 23, 27, 29, 31, 37, 43, 45, 47, 51, 53, 61, 63, 67, 69, 71, 73, 75, 85, 89, 97, 99, 101, 109, 113, 115, 119, 123, 127, 133, 135, 143, 145, 147, 149, 153, 157, 165, 169
sunset 33, 41, 55, 79, 105, 115, 117, 137, 151
sword 49, 121, 141, 167, 168, 177, 178

T

Tetragrammaton. 172, 174, 176, 178, 186, 187, 188
tin 21, 39, 57, 59, 87, 125, 155
triangle 42, 83, 104, 144, 170, 172, 177, 178, 179, 182, 183, 186, 187, 188, 189, 190
twilight 25, 35, 49, 65, 77, 81, 111, 121, 129, 131, 139

U

Ualac .... See Volac
Umabel 138
Uvall 109

V

Valak .... See Volac
Valefor 27

valerian 164
Valu .... See Volac
Vapula 135
Vashariah 80
Vassago 21
Vehuel 114
Vehuiah 17
Vepar 99
vervain 164
Vevaliah 102
Vine 105
Volac 139
Voso .... See Ose

W

wand 42, 169, 177, 178, 179, 184, 186, 189
water 163
West 41, 43, 45, 47, 51, 89, 91, 95, 97, 99, 137, 139, 141, 143, 145, 147

Y

Yabamiah 156
Yahehel 140
Yechuiah 82
Yeiael 60
Yeialel 132
Yeiazel 96
Yelahiah 104
Yerathel 70
Yesod 14
Yezalel 42

Z

Zagan 137
Zepar 47
Ziminiar 29, 31, 33, 35, 37, 39, 77, 79, 81, 83, 85, 87, 125, 127, 129, 131, 133, 135
Zodiac 14

FOUNDATIONS OF PRACTICAL SORCERY

A seven-volume set of magical treatises, unabridged, comprising:

Vol. I - Liber Noctis

A Handbook of the Sorcerous Arte

Liber Noctis explores the attitudes, training and preparation required for success in ritual, and, as the title suggests, does not shy away from the 'darker' aspects of magic. Practical, experiential, lucid and non-judgmental, this book lays the groundwork for the successful study and practice of sorcery in the modern world.

Vol. II - Ars Salomonis

Being of that Hidden Arte of Solomon the King

Ars Salomonis is a practical manual for working with the talismanic figures found in the Key of Solomon, the most significant of all grimoires. Including two methods for empowering and activating the planetary pentacles, the author makes this vital work safely accessible to beginners. It is an ideal entranceway into the grimoire tradition.

Vol. III - Ars Geomantica

Being an account and rendition of the Arte of Geomantic Divination and Magic

Ars Geomantica explores the medieval system of Geomancy, one of the simplest and most practical of the divinatory arts. The inclusion of detailed instructions on the creation of geomantic staves, elemental fluid condensers, and talismanic construction and consecration make this work a superb introduction to an extensive assortment of magical and divinatory principles.

Vol. IV - Ars Theurgia Goetia

Being an account and rendition of the Arte and Praxis of the Conjuration of some of the Spirits of Solomon

Ars Theurgia Goetia presents a precise and practical guide to working with the spirits of this neglected text from the Solomonic grimoire cycle, the Theurgia-Goetia, giving the full seals of the spirits for the first time. The complete ritual sequence of preparation, conjuration, and license to depart is lucidly demonstrated, making this work suitable for both the beginner and the experienced practitioner.

Vol. V - Otz Chim

The Tree of Life

Otz Chim is a practical exploration of the magic of the Kabbalistic Tree of Life, the glyph that concentrates the essence of magic and mysticism within the Western Mystery Tradition. This book focuses on lesser-known aspects such as the angels associated with the paths, their seals, and invocations and includes the previously unavailable Massa Aborum Vitae.

Vol. VI - Ars Speculum

Being an Instruction on the Arte of using Mirrors and Shewstones in Magic

Ars Speculum is a concise and practical work on the use of mirrors and shewstones in magic. In it the author explores skrying and working with the four elements of air, fire, water and earth - both with elemental condensers and different elemental creatures. Other techniques include contacting other levels of being, the conjuration of spirits, binding and ligature, and healing and protection.

Vol. VII - Liber Terriblis

Being an Instruction on the seventy-two Spirits of the Goetia

Liber Terribilis is a practical study of how to work with the seventy-two spirits of the infamous seventeenth-century Grimoire, the Goetia. It also explores the vital and often neglected use of the seventy-two binding angels of the Great Name of God, the Schemhamphorasch. This volume will be of value to all levels of students and practitioners of the grimoire traditions, being based upon the work of a small group of occultists who have explored it in practice.

More information available on the Avalonia website-
www.avaloniabooks.co.uk

Or write to:
BM Avalonia
London
WC1N 3XX
England, United Kingdom

Expanding the Esoteric Horizons ...

Avalonia *is an independent publisher producing outstanding and innovative books which push the boundaries of their subjects and illuminate the spirit of the sacred in its many manifestations.*

Explore some of the other works on the occult, mythology and magic published by Avalonia at:

www.avaloniabooks.co.uk

Readers who found Foundations of Practical Sorcery of interest, is likely to enjoy:

A Collection of Magical Secrets & a Treatise of mixed Cabalah by Stephen Skinner and David Rankine

Climbing the Tree of Life by David Rankine

Living Theurgy by Jeffrey S. Kupperman

Practical Elemental Magick by Sorita d'Este and David Rankine

The Book of Gold by David Rankine & Paul Harry Barron (trans.)

The Book of Treasure Spirits, edited by David Rankine

The Complete Grimoire of Pope Honorius by David Rankine & Paul Harry Barron (trans.)

The Cunning Man's Handbook by Jim Baker

The Grimoire of Arthur Gauntlet by David Rankine

Thoth by Lesley Jackson

Thracian Magic by Georgi Mishev

Wicca Magickal Beginnings by Sorita d'Este and David Rankine

www.ingramcontent.com/pod-product-compliance
Lightning Source LLC
Chambersburg PA
CBHW032044150426

43194CB00006B/419